coming to me: W9-BLC-129

9/5/23

You're following the
heart of God.

9/23/23

He also, wrote book
called

Not By Sight
"See, taplet"

"Let's Seek the heart of God!"

GOD'S WAYS ARE NOT YOUR WAYS

Don't Follow Your Heart

JON BLOOM

Don't Follow Your Heart: God's Ways Are Not Your Ways

Copyright © 2015 by Desiring God

Download this book in three digital formats, free of charge, at desiringGod.org

Published by Desiring God
     Post Office Box 2901
     Minneapolis, MN 55402

ISBN: 978-0-9912776-8-1
Cover design: Christopher Tobias, Tobias' Outerwear for Books
eBook design: Josh Pritchard, Gideon House Books
Typesetting: Ryan Leichty
First printing 2015
Printed in the United States of America

For my mother,
Marilyn Judith Berglund Bloom

You did not follow your heart.
Instead, you directed your heart to love.

CONTENTS

A WORD TO
THE READER

THIS IS A BOOK to help you with heart problems. Because your biggest problems in life are heart problems. And they often occur because you begin to follow your heart's direction rather than direct your heart. So this book is to help you "be wise, and direct your heart in the way" (Prov. 23:19).

God considered David a man after his own heart (1 Sam. 13:14). Stephen gave us insight into what God meant: "I have found in David the son of Jesse a man after my heart, who will do all my will" (Acts 13:22). What qualified David to be king was that he followed God's heart. And when he did, he did very well.

But when David didn't follow God's heart, he did not do well. When David followed his own heart he was on his way to slaughter Nabal and his household, and only Abigail's quick thinking and wise intervention saved David from this bloodguilt (1 Sam. 25:32–34). When David followed his own heart, he slept with Bathsheba, robbing her of her chastity and Uriah of his wife and life (2 Sam. 11), and brought devastating evil into his household (2 Samuel 12). When David followed his own heart, he took a census that God had said not to take and it resulted in seventy thousand deaths (1 Chronicles 21).

The Bible is full of examples that warn us not to follow our hearts. When Moses followed his heart, he killed an Egyptian (Ex. 2:12) and faithlessly struck the rock (Num. 20:10–12). When Balaam followed his heart, he was rebuked by a donkey (Num. 22:30). When Nebuchadnezzar followed his heart, he ended up eating grass like an ox (Dan. 4:32). When Haman followed his heart, he ended up hanging from the gallows he had built (Est. 7:10). When the disciples followed their hearts, they argued over who was the greatest (Luke 9:46) and in terror abandoned Jesus in Gethsemane (Matt. 26:56). When Ananias and Sapphira followed their hearts, they lied to the Holy Spirit and dropped dead (Acts 5:1–11).

The Bible is clear: we must follow God's heart, not ours. Today, following God's heart means to follow Jesus, which means dying to our fallen hearts' desires and losing our lives in order to find them (Matt. 16:24–25).

My prayer is that this book will help you follow Jesus by resisting your heart's errant predilections and directing it to do all God's will. It contains thirty-one meditations, so you can use it as a month-long heart recalibration assistant if you wish, but this book is not a program. It's not "Thirty-One Days to a New Heart." It is simply a collection of helps for common heart problems. The order of the short chapters is meant to be helpful to you, but if it is not, you can read them in the way that you find most helpful.

Following God's heart is no easy thing. Because sin infects our hearts, his ways are often not our ways (Isa. 55:9). He frequently leads us down paths that look strange to us and sometimes plain wrong. May this book help guide you during confusing turns and point you to the light when the path seems dark (Ps. 119:105).

Jon Bloom
desiringGod.org
Minneapolis, Minnesota

*The heart is deceitful above all things, and
desperately sick; who can understand it?*

JEREMIAH 17:9

DON'T FOLLOW YOUR HEART

"FOLLOW YOUR HEART" IS a creed embraced by billions of people. It's a statement of faith in one of the great pop-cultural myths of the Western world—a gospel proclaimed in many of our stories, movies, and songs.

Essentially, it's a belief that your heart is a compass inside of you that will direct you to your own true north if you just have the courage to follow it. It says that your heart is a true guide that will lead you to true happiness if you just have the courage to listen to it. The creed says that you are lost and your heart will save you.

This creed can sound so simple and beautiful and liberating. For lost people it's a tempting gospel to believe.

Is This the Leader You Want to Follow?

Until you consider that your heart has sociopathic tendencies. Think about it for a moment. What does your heart tell you?

Please don't answer. Your heart has likely said things today that you would not wish to repeat. I know mine has. My heart tells me that all of reality ought to serve my desires. My heart likes to think the best of me and worst of others, unless those others happen to think well of me—then they are wonderful people. But if they don't think well of me, or even if they just disagree with me, well then, something must be wrong with them. And while my heart is pondering my virtues and others' errors, it can suddenly find some immoral or horribly angry thought very attractive.

The "follow your heart" creed certainly isn't found in the Bible. The Bible actually thinks our hearts have a disease: "The heart is deceitful above all things, and desperately sick; who can understand it?" (Jer. 17:9). Jesus, the great physician, lists the grim symptoms of this disease: "Out of the heart come evil thoughts, murder, adultery, sexual immorality, theft, false witness, slander" (Matt. 15:19). This is not leadership material.

The truth is, no one lies to us more than our own hearts. No one. If our hearts are compasses, they are Jack Sparrow compasses.[1] They don't tell us the truth; they just tell us what we want. If our hearts are guides, they are Gothels.[2] They are not benevolent; they are pathologically selfish. In fact, if we do what our hearts tell us to do, we will pervert and impoverish every desire, every beauty, every person, every wonder, and every joy. Our hearts want to consume these things for our own self-glory and self-indulgence.

No, our hearts will not save us. We need to be saved from our hearts.

---

1   Jack Sparrow, a fictional character in Walt Disney Pictures' *Pirates of the Caribbean* major motion-picture series, possesses a compass that points to whatever its owner desires most.
2   Mother Gothel is a fictional character in Walt Disney Pictures' animated film *Tangled* (2010), who dishonestly and manipulatively "guides" Rapunzel for Gothel's own narcissistic ends.

This Is the Leader You Want to Follow

Our hearts were never designed to be followed, but to be led. Our hearts were never designed to be gods in whom we believe; they were designed to believe in God.

If we make our hearts gods and ask them to lead us, they will lead us to narcissistic misery and ultimately damnation. They cannot save us, because what's wrong with our hearts is the heart of our problem. But if our hearts believe in God, as they are designed to, then God saves us (Heb. 7:25) and leads our hearts to exceeding joy (Ps. 43:4).

Therefore, don't believe in your heart; direct your heart to believe in God. Don't follow your heart; follow Jesus. Note that Jesus did not say to his disciples, "Let not your hearts be troubled, just believe in your hearts." He said, "Let not your hearts be troubled. Believe in God; believe also in me" (John 14:1).

So though your heart will try to shepherd you today, do not follow it. It is not a shepherd. It is a pompous sheep that, due to remaining sin, has some wolf-like qualities. Don't follow it, and be careful even listening to it.

Remember, your heart only tells you what you want, not where you should go. So only listen to it to note what it's telling you about what you want, and then take your wants, both good and evil, to Jesus as requests and confessions.

Jesus is your shepherd (Ps. 23:1; John 10:14). Listen to his voice in his word and follow him (John 10:27). Let him be, in the words of a great hymn, the "heart of

[your] own heart whatever befall."[3] He is the truth, he is the way, and he will lead you to life (John 14:6).

---

3   From the eighth-century hymn "Be Thou My Vision," trans. Eleanor Hull (1912).

Trust in the L<small>ORD</small> with all your heart, and do not lean on your own understanding. In all your ways acknowledge him, and he will make straight your paths.

PROVERBS 3:5-6

2

THE INSANITY OF LEANING ON OUR OWN UNDERSTANDING

WHEN THE BIBLE TELLS us not to lean on our own understanding (Prov. 3:5), it is not encouraging us to be irrational. The Bible puts up no wall of separation between our intellect and faith. In fact, the book of Proverbs speaks very highly of understanding:

- "[Incline] your heart to understanding." (2:2)
- "Raise your voice for understanding." (2:3)
- "Understanding will guard you." (2:11)
- "Blessed is the one who . . . gets understanding." (3:13)
- "Wisdom rests in the heart of a man of understanding." (14:33)
- "The heart of him who has understanding seeks knowledge." (15:14)
- "To get understanding is to be chosen rather than silver." (16:16)
- "Buy wisdom, instruction, and understanding." (23:23)

So if we're supposed to get understanding, why are we not supposed to lean on it?

Note carefully what Proverbs 3:5 tells us not to lean on: our *own* understanding. In other words, we are not to lean on conclusions we deduce primarily from our perceptions. In this sense, our own understanding simply will not bear the full weight of reality. It was never intended to.

The Insanity of Trusting Ourselves

Let's go back to the garden of Eden. The one tree in the garden from which humans were forbidden to eat was not, interestingly, the Tree of Life (Gen. 2:9). It was not life that God denied human beings. He forbade them to eat from the Tree of the Knowledge of Good and Evil (Gen. 2:17).

The point of this prohibition was not to keep humans ignorant but, as John Piper says, "to preserve [for us] the pleasures of the world."[4] It was as if God was saying,

> If you eat of that one [tree] you will be saying to me, "I'm smarter than you. I am more authoritative than you. I am wiser than you are. I think I can care for myself better than you care for me. You are not a very good Father. And so I am going to reject you." So don't eat from the tree,

---

4 John Piper, "Why Did God Forbid One Tree in Eden?," *Desiring God* website, October 18, 2013, accessed September 12, 2015, http://www.desiringgod.org/articles/why-did-god-forbid-one-tree-in-eden.

because you will be rejecting me and all my
good gifts and all my wisdom and all my care.
Instead, keep on submitting to my will. Keep on
affirming my wisdom. Keep on being thankful
for my generosity. Keep on trusting me as a Father and keep on eating from these [other] trees
as a way of enjoying me.[5]

You see, in order to handle the knowledge of good and
evil, a person must possess (1) the ability to completely
comprehend all possible options and contingencies (omniscience); (2) the righteousness and wisdom to choose
the right course; and (3) the power to make reality conform to the right course (omnipotence).

In other words, only God can handle such
knowledge.

What this means is that it is not the one who trusts
in the Lord who is irrational, but the one who leans on
his or her own understanding. It is insane to trust such
pitifully limited understanding when one can trust the
unlimited understanding of God.

The Joyful Sanity of Trusting the Lord

So many of the things that cause us the most difficulty
and heartache in life, the source of so much of our anxiety, fear, doubt, and anger with others and with God, is
the result of leaning on our own understanding.

God does not want us to be miserable, even in this
fallen, futility infected evil age. He wants to relieve our

5   Ibid.

anxiety (Luke 12:11–12; Phil. 4:6–7), fear (Ps. 118:6; 1 Pet. 3:6), doubt (Matt. 21:21; Luke 24:38), and sinful anger (Eph. 4:31). And so he gives us Proverbs 3:5–6 as a priceless gift.

In exercising faith—trusting fully in the Lord and not leaning on our own understanding—we're not setting aside our intellect. We're resting our intellect upon the intellect of God. Nothing is wiser or saner. To do so is to allow him to direct our paths, which not only lead to ultimate joy but also make the journey itself, even when laden with sorrow, joyful (2 Cor. 6:10). And it preserves for us all the pleasures God provides us in the world. To not do this is the height of foolishness and the path to misery.

So let us choose joy today by not leaning on our own understanding, but in sweet, childlike faith let us trust the sure, firm foundation of our loving Creator's omniscience.

As for you, you meant evil against me, but God meant it for good, to bring it about that many people should be kept alive, as they are today.

GENESIS 50:20

3

HOW INVOLVED IS GOD IN THE DETAILS OF YOUR LIFE?

WHY DOES GOD GIVE us more details about Joseph's life than any other individual in Genesis?

Genesis has an interesting structure. It zooms over the creation account (about 3 percent of the book) like a rocket, soars over the millennia between Adam and Abraham (about 15 percent—dropping speed and altitude over Noah) like a jet, and cruises over Abraham (21 percent), Isaac (8 percent), and Jacob (23 percent) like a helicopter, hovering here and there. Then it sort of drives down the road of Joseph's life, devoting to it nearly 30 percent of its content.

God is always intentional in his proportionality. *More* does not necessarily equal *more important* in God's word economy. The epistle to the Ephesians is much shorter than the narrative of Joseph's life, but it is not less important. However, more does imply *take note.* There are crucial things God wants us to see.

God has many reasons to drive us through Joseph's life, some more obvious than others. Let's look at one perhaps less obvious reason.

Sightings of Sovereignty in the Life of Joseph

On this drive, if we're paying attention to the scenery out the windows, we see a startling and unnerving level of God's providential involvement in the details of Joseph's life. Here are some of the scenes (warning: some of these scenes you may find disturbing):

- Joseph's place in the patriarchal birth order was part of God's plan (Gen. 30:22–24).
- This means Rachel's agonizing struggle with infertility was part of God's plan (30:1–2).
- Jacob's romantic preference of Rachel and therefore his (probably paternally insensitive) favoritism shown to Joseph was part of God's plan (29:30; 37:3).
- Joseph's prophetic dreams were (obviously) part of God's plan (37:5–11).
- His brothers' jealousy (note: sibling rivalry and family conflict) was part of God's plan (37:8).
- His brothers' evil, murderous, greedy betrayal of him, and Judah's part in it, was part of God's plan (37:18–28; 50:20).
- His brothers' twenty-plus–year deception of Jacob regarding Joseph was part of God's plan.
- The existence of an evil slave trade at the time was part of God's plan (37:26–27).
- Potiphar's complicity with the slave trade and his position in Egypt was part of God's plan (37:36).
- Joseph's extraordinary administrative gifting was part of God's plan (39:2–4).
- Joseph's favor with Potiphar was part of God's plan (39:4–6).

- Potiphar's wife's being given over to sexual immorality was part of God's plan (Gen. 39:8–12; Rom. 1:24).
- Potiphar's wife's dishonesty was part of God's plan (Gen. 39:14–18).
- Potiphar's unjust judgment of Joseph was part of God's plan (39:19–20).
- The particular prison Joseph was sent to—the one that would receive the cupbearer and the baker—was part of God's plan (39:20).
- Joseph's favor with the prison warden was part of God's plan (39:21–23).
- The high-level conspiracy against Pharaoh and its exposure resulting in the imprisonment of Pharaoh's cupbearer and baker were part of God's plan (40:1–3).
- Joseph being appointed to care for the cupbearer and baker was part of God's plan (40:4).
- The dreams the cupbearer and baker had were (obviously) part of God's plan (40:5).
- Joseph's compassionate concern for their troubled hearts was part of God's plan (40:6–7).
- Their trusting Joseph's integrity enough to confide their dreams in him was part of God's plan (40:8–20).
- Joseph's discerning the meaning of their dreams was part of God's plan (40:12–13, 18–19).
- The Egyptian judicial processes that exonerated the cupbearer and condemned the baker were part of God's plan (40:20–22).
- The cupbearer failing to remember Joseph for two years was part of God's plan (40:23–41:1).

- The timing of Pharaoh's dreams was part of God's plan (41:1–7).
- The inability of Pharaoh's counselors to discern his dreams was part of God's plan (41:8).
- The cupbearer remembering Joseph and having the courage to remind Pharaoh of an event that might re-arouse suspicion was part of God's plan (41:9–13).
- Pharaoh's being desperate enough to listen to a Hebrew prisoner was part of God's plan (41:14–15).
- Joseph's having discernment of Pharaoh's dreams was part of God's plan (41:25–36).
- The miraculous amount of immediate trust that Pharaoh placed in Joseph's interpretation and counsel was part of God's plan (41:37–40).
- Joseph's being given Asenath (an Egyptian) for a wife was part of God's plan (41:45).
- Joseph's two sons by Asenath, Manasseh and Ephraim, were part of God's plan (41:50–52; 48:5).
- The complex confluence of natural phenomena that caused the extraordinarily fruitful years followed by the extraordinarily desolate years, with all the resulting human prosperity and suffering, and the consolidation of Egyptian wealth and power in Pharaoh's hands were part of God's plan (41:53–57; 47:13–26).
- The threat of starvation that caused terrible hardship and fear and moved Jacob to send his sons to Egypt for grain was part of God's plan (42:1–2).
- The brothers' safe journey to Egypt and Benjamin's nonparticipation was part of God's plan (42:3–4).

- The brothers' bowing to Joseph in unwitting fulfillment of the dreams they had hated was part of God's plan (42:6).
- Joseph's whole scheme to test his brothers was part of God's plan (42:9–44:34).
- Simeon's being chosen to remain in Egypt was part of God's plan (42:24).
- Jacob's refusal to release Benjamin to return to Egypt causing the delay of the brothers' return and Simeon's bewildering experience in custody was part of God's plan (42:38).
- The relentless threat of starvation that prompted Judah to make his personal guarantee of Benjamin's safe return and forced Jacob to finally allow Benjamin go to Egypt was part of God's plan (43:8–14).
- The success with which Joseph was able to continue to conceal his identity and pull off the framing of Benjamin for thievery and all the anguish the brothers experienced as a result were part of God's plan (43:15–44:17).
- Judah's willingness to exchange his life for Benjamin's out of love for his father, and thus initiating his own sale into slavery, like he had initiated Joseph's sale into slavery, was part of God's plan (44:18–34).
- Joseph's timing in revealing himself to his brothers was part of God's plan (45:1–14).
- Jacob's being told by his sons of Joseph's survival and position in Egypt and, consequently, the exposure of his other sons' twenty-plus–year deceit regarding Joseph's disappearance and all the ac-

companying relational pain were part of God's plan
(45:25–28).

- God's directing Jacob to move to Egypt was (obviously) part of God's plan (46:2–4).
- The relocation of the entire clan of Israel to Egypt, where they would reside and grow for 430 years and eventually become horribly enslaved, thus fulfilling God's promise to Abraham in Genesis 15:13–14, was part of God's plan (46:5–47:12).

If we wished, there are more sightings we could include from this drive. But these give us a lot to chew on.

Joseph's Life and Yours

Joseph had a unique role to play in redemptive history. But God's intricate involvement in Joseph's life is not unique to him. God is just as involved in the details of our lives. One of the many reasons God gives us a close-up of Joseph's life is to show us how active he is, how he never leaves us or forsakes us all along the way, in both the good and the evil things we experience (Heb. 13:5).

Joseph knew God's nearness when he woke from his prophetic dreams and probably when he experienced remarkable favor. But how near did God feel to Joseph in the pit of his brothers' betrayal, or shackled in the Ishmaelite caravan, or when falsely accused of attempted rape, or stuck for years in the king's prison, forgotten? Yet we see that God was there all the time working all things together for good for Joseph and millions of others (Rom. 8:28).

Yes, God was even working the evil, heinous things people did to Joseph for good. We can say that, because that's precisely what Joseph himself said to his brothers about their betrayal of him: "As for you, you meant evil against me, but God meant it for good, to bring it about that many people should be kept alive, as they are today" (Gen. 50:20).

The detailed narrative of Joseph's life, among many other things, is a loving letter from your Good Shepherd (John 10:11)—the same Good Shepherd who guided Joseph through green pastures and the valley of the shadow of death, pursuing him with good all the days of his life (Ps. 23:1–6)—to remind you that no matter what you are experiencing, sweet or bitter, good or evil, no matter how long it's lasting, he has not left you alone (John 14:18). He is with you (Ps. 23:4), he is working all things together for good (Rom. 8:28), and he will be with you to the end (Matt. 28:20).

*The secret things belong to the L*ORD *our God, but the things that are revealed belong to us and to our children forever.*

DEUTERONOMY 29:29

GOD'S BRIGHT DESIGN FOR YOUR BITTER PROVIDENCES

GOD TELLS US EVERYTHING we need to know to live godly lives (2 Pet. 1:3). But sometimes we wonder.

"God Moves in a Mysterious Way"[6]

The unexpected, unexplained twists and turns our lives take create all kinds of apparent uncertainties for us. And the profound pain we endure can be so perplexing. There is so much God doesn't tell us—so much we think we would really like to know.

But as Deuteronomy 29:29 says, "The secret things belong to the LORD our God, but the things that are revealed belong to us and to our children forever."

This means that as creatures we must learn to live contentedly with what God intends to be mysterious to us and grab hold of the revealed things with everything we have.

---

6 The section headers in this chapter are quotes from William Cowper's famous hymn "God Moves in a Mysterious Way" (1774).

"Deep in Unfathomable Mines"

The secrets God keeps from us are a greater mercy to us than we likely realize. We often forget just how thin is the sliver of reality we see and the information we can contain at any given time. Humans are not equipped to handle what the Bible calls "the knowledge of good and evil" (Gen. 2:17).

When we want God to start giving us some answers, we need the Bible to help us get our heads out of the claustrophobic confines of our private worlds and into the galactic greatness of what he is letting us be a part of. We need to remember that we're dealing with God here.

God is a person for whom time, space, and matter present no limitations. He has dimensions accessible to him that we know nothing about. He is Trinitarian in his essence (Matt. 28:19). He holds tens (maybe hundreds) of billions of galaxies together by the word of his power (Heb. 1:3). He has created and governs every throne, dominion, ruler, and authority (Col. 1:16) and every being that is invisible to us, whether angel (Rom. 8:38) or demon (Luke 4:41).

He is orchestrating all of human history (Acts 17:26) with its multiple billions of complex individuals past, present, and future—of which each of us is only one—and multiple trillions of interweaving causes and effects—of which each of us only experiences a relative handful. And he's working all of these things toward a point when every knee will bow and every tongue will confess that Jesus Christ is Lord to the glory of God the Father (Phil. 2:9–11).

And we wonder why we struggle to understand what God is doing in our difficult circumstances.

"He Treasures Up His Bright Designs"

God is doing ten thousand things in our circumstances! That's likely a significant underestimate.

We would fall on our faces in awe-filled worship if we saw the chain reaction for our eternal good (Rom. 8:28) and that of other present and future believers that God is engineering in just one seemingly random occurrence (Prov. 16:33) that today might be the source of our grumbling because of the grief it is causing us. Now think of a lifetime's worth.

God doesn't explicitly promise this, but I tend to think that one of the glories and joys of the age to come will be God's unveiling of the bright, extensive designs of his bitter providences in this age and the grace upon grace upon grace that they unleashed while we, not knowing, simply held on to Proverbs 3:5–6 with all our might.

"His Purposes Will Ripen Fast"

But what God does explicitly promise is that every moment and level of suffering we experience as we live by faith (Rom. 1:17) "is preparing for us an eternal weight of glory beyond all comparison" (2 Cor. 4:17).

That thing that you don't want, that you're weary of, that you plead with God to remove—and might remove at some point unless he says otherwise (2 Cor. 12:9)—is preparing you for glory.

God's will for you is your sanctification (1 Thess. 4:3). He wants you to share his holiness (Heb. 12:10). And the kindness of God in pursuing this for you is incomprehensively wonderful, because without his holiness you will have no real and lasting happiness. Only in his presence is fullness of joy (Ps. 16:11), and only the pure in heart will see him (Matt. 5:8).

You want him to make you holy. You really do. Whatever it takes.

"Ye Fearful Saints, Fresh Courage Take"

The God who governs the visible and invisible worlds knows what he is doing in your life. The God who was brutally murdered on a Roman cross knows what it's like to suffer and how to redeem it. Specifically how he will bring good out of your trials may be mysterious to you now, but that he will bring good out of them is not a mystery. It's a promise.

And this is where you get to participate with God in your sanctification! You get to act the miracle. You work out your salvation (Phil. 2:12) by believing the promises God makes to you (John 6:29).

And as you believe God's promises, you will bear the "peaceful fruit of righteousness" (Heb. 12:11), which are the attitudes and actions of those who live by faith in the Son of God (Gal. 2:20). Behavior always follows belief. So your belief will result in faith-filled obedience to God (Rom. 1:5) and produce various kinds of faith-fueled works for God (2 Thess. 1:11).

The secret things are the Lord's for a very good reason. Trust him with the mystery. But the revealed things are yours, and they are glorious. Believe them, and one day you'll share God's holiness and all the forevermore pleasures he has prepared for you (Ps. 16:11).

Therefore, my beloved . . . work out your own salvation
with fear and trembling, for it is God who works in
you, both to will and to work for his good pleasure.

PHILIPPIANS 2:12–13

GOD IS AT WORK IN YOUR UNREMARKABLE DAYS

I OFTEN BEGIN A calendar year reading in Genesis as I embark on a one-year journey through the greatest, most influential book ever published in human history. I have spent my entire adult life reading and studying the Bible, and at age fifty (as I write this), I feel like I may be in about the third grade in mastery. That is likely giving myself too much credit.

This Book enlightens and confounds, humbles and encourages me. It has more wisdom in it than can possibly be mined in a lifetime. It speaks to me in the things that it explicitly says and also in what it doesn't say.

And what stood out to me on my most recent trek through Genesis was the remarkable work of God in the unremarkable years—all the years stretching between God's recorded historical in-breakings.

The Unremarkable Years of Genesis

Genesis covers an incredible span of time. The most conservative evangelical scholars estimate the time between Adam and Abraham at between two thousand and six thousand years (possible gaps in the genealogies being the variable), which means, at minimum, Genesis

alone covers approximately the same amount of historical time as the rest of the books of the Bible combined,
and possibly much more.

And what do we know about those millennia?
Remarkably little, when you think about it. After the
creation of Adam and Eve (chapters 1–2), we learn about
the fall (chapter 3), and about Cain's murder of Abel
(chapter 4), and then we are provided only genealogies
with a few historical remarks tossed in until we get to
Noah. How many years passed between Adam and Noah
(chapters 2–5)? A minimum of sixteen hundred years,
possibly much more.

Between Noah and Abraham (chapters 6–11) there
are centuries (about 350 years minimum, possibly much
more). And besides the flood account, the only things
the Bible tells us about these years are a few events
regarding Noah and his sons, more genealogies, and the
story of the Tower of Babel.

Then with Abraham, Isaac, Jacob, and the patriarchs
(chapters 12–50), Genesis begins to give us a lot more
information. Although, considering that these thir-
ty-nine chapters span about 360 years, most of those
years also go without comment.

God Does Not Waste Time or People

Now, just for the sake of rough calculation and some
contemplation, let's assume about two thousand years
between Adam and Abraham, and let's assume solar
years (365 days). That would be approximately 730,000
days that passed with only a handful of them containing
events that God decided to record.

What was God doing during all those unremarkable days—years we know nothing about when people were "eating and drinking and marrying and being given in marriage . . . [and] buying and selling, planting and building" (Luke 17:27–28)—all those years of wonders and horrors, some of which we've unearthed in archeological tells? Were they just throwaway years and disposable people?

No. Every single one of those 730,000 days was a unique, priceless, irreplaceable creation of God's (Ps. 118:24). And every single person was a unique, priceless, irreplaceable creation of God's, each bearing God's image (Gen. 1:27), however marred and distorted. Each had a unique story; each played a role in the Great Story whether for good or ill (Rom. 9:21). Each had meaning to God. He knew them intimately, though they lived and died anonymous to us. Each one's destiny, whether resulting in mercy or judgment, we entrust to the judge of all the earth who only does what is just (Gen. 18:25). Many wasted their lives, but God did not waste theirs.

God was not wasting time or people during these unrecorded days. He was holding all things together by the word of his power every moment (Col. 1:17; Heb. 1:3), and he was working in every detail of history and human experience (John 5:17; Acts 17:26–28) so that in the fullness of time he might enter history and human experience as the second Adam and complete his plan to redeem what had fallen on that horrible, remarkable day in the garden (Gal. 4:4–5; Rom. 5:17). God was not absent or deistically distant (Acts 17:27–28); neither was he silent (Rom. 1:20).

God Does Not Waste Your Time or You

Let the unremarkable days of Genesis speak to you. A few days of your life are remarkable, containing events and experiences where you see God's providence with startling clarity and when your faith and life course are indelibly and memorably shaped. But the vast majority of your days—likely a day like today—will pass into obscurity, unrecorded and irretrievable to your memory. But though today may be unremarkable, it is not unimportant. It is unique, priceless, and irreplaceable.

Today God is at work in you both to will and to work for his good pleasure (Phil. 2:13). Today God is at work in you to advance toward completion the good work that he began in you (Phil. 1:6). Today, though unseen and unfelt by you, God is at work in every detail of your history and experience and the history and experience of possibly thousands of others, to bring about answers to your long-requested prayers, to open the door that seems impossibly closed to you, to turn the prodigal homeward, to save your hard-hearted loved one, to deliver you from the affliction, or to make you an unexpected, remarkable means of grace to someone else.

Today is a day that the Lord has specially made (Ps. 118:24). He has planned it for you. It has a purpose. No matter what it holds, give thanks for it (1 Thess. 5:18). For God does not waste a day, and he will not waste you. And if you love and trust him, you will one day discover that today, unremarkable as it now seems, will do you remarkable good (Rom. 8:28).

I am the vine; you are the branches.

JOHN 15:5

6

GOD LOVES GOOD WINE

GOD LIKES USING WINES and vines in his miracles and parables. I thought of that a number of years ago when I read the following in an article:

> Great wines come from low-yielding vineyards planted in marginal climates on the poorest soils. Though hard on the vines, these tough conditions are good for the wine, because the vines that are stressed must work harder to produce fruit, which leads to fewer but more concentrated and flavorful grapes.
>
> By contrast, the vines used for bulk wines have it easy. They are planted in the fertile soils in ideal climates of regions such as California's Central Valley. Such regions are great for producing tons of grapes to fill up the bulk fermentation tanks, but not at all great for producing the complex, intense flavors needed to make great wine, because the vines are not stressed and the yields are way too high.[7]

7 Ben Giliberti, "It's Not the Box, It's the Bulk," *Washington Post*, July 20, 2005, accessed September 26, 2015, http://www.washingtonpost.com/wp-dyn/content/article/2005/07/19/AR2005071900312.html.

Stressed vines produce good wines. This phenomenon of nature is also a parable for how God produces rich, complex, intense faith in his children. Because when it comes to faith, God loves good wine.

All you have to do is read Hebrews 11 to see that the great wine of faith often "comes from . . . vineyards planted in marginal climates on the poorest soils." And James 1:2 tells us plainly that "tough conditions ("various trials") are good for the wine" of faith. That's because faith-vines "must work harder to produce fruit" leading to "more concentrated and flavorful" wines.

Now, as a faith vine striving to grow in a hard place, you might be tempted to wish you were a bulk-wine vine basking in the spiritual equivalent of California's Central Valley. O, for that rich soil, bright sunshine, warm ocean air. Sigh. But here you are, stuck on some coldish, semi-arid hillside where the struggle is frequent and sometimes severe.

Yes, it's hard. But it's not a mistake. It's not a punishment. It's not mean. It's simply that tough conditions produce the best faith. Your vinedresser (John 15:1) has planted you in a unique vineyard with uniquely stressful conditions because he intends for you to produce a uniquely fine, flavorful faith wine. And he will tend to your every real need (Phil. 4:19).

If you need some perspective today, review Hebrews 11 and the great faith-vine heroes of history. Remember what their vineyards were like and the rich faith wines that resulted. And then remember Jesus (Heb. 12:2) and the joy set before every vine that endures in faith.

When God makes wine, he makes really good wine (John 2:7–10). And when it comes to your faith, he knows that really good wine is made in the vineyard.

Do all things without grumbling or disputing, that you may be blameless and innocent, children of God without blemish in the midst of a crooked and twisted generation, among whom you shine as lights in the world.

PHILIPPIANS 2:14–15

7

WE ARE FAR TOO EASILY DISPLEASED

I AM A GRUMBLER by (fallen) nature.

Just this morning a malfunctioning software program required my attention. Experience told me the likely course: at least two times on the phone with customer support and at least two glitches in the fixing process. Forty-five minutes minimum. Probably more. (All proved true, by the way.) Immediately I resented this time-stealing inconvenience. And when my wife called in the middle of dealing with it, out of my mouth came my displeasure.

Life problems don't get much smaller. What is the matter with me?

The matter is that I too easily listen to the lies of my pathologically selfish sin nature, which assumes all of reality should serve my preferences and grumbles against anything that doesn't. The truth is, when I grumble, I have lost touch with reality.

What Grumbling Gauges

Grumbling is a gauge of the human soul. It gauges our gaze on grace. It tells us that we're not seeing grace.

Grumbling pours out of our soul whenever we feel like we're not getting what we deserve. Sometimes we're even crass enough to think, *To hell with what we deserve; we're not getting what we want.*

Grumbling is a symptom of a myopic soul. Selfishness has caused tunnel vision and has fixated on a craving. The soul has lost sight of the glory and wonder and splendor and hope that is the reborn, redeemed life, and thus it is far too easily displeased. Grumbling is evidence of soul-vision impairment.

What Gratitude Gauges

The opposite of grumbling in the soul is gratitude. And gratitude also gauges our gaze on grace. It tells us that we are seeing grace.

Gratitude pours out of our souls whenever we're receiving a gift we know we don't deserve and we experience a humble happiness. And as sinners who have received the gospel of the grace of God (Acts 20:24), we are receiving these gifts *all the time.*

Gratitude is a symptom of a healthy, expansive soul. The gospel of grace has given it panoramic vision, allowing it to see that this grace will be sufficient (2 Cor. 12:9) to meet every need (Phil. 4:19) when inconvenience, crisis, weakness, affliction, unexpected demand, suffering, and persecution hit. In fact, in all these things this grace will make us "more than conquerors through him who loved us" (Rom. 8:37).

Accents of Heaven and Hell

Gratitude is the accent of the language of heaven, because there *everything* is undeserved grace. No creature that basks in the eternal, deep, powerful, satisfying, overflowing joys of heaven will have merited being there. Each will be there solely by the grace of God, which is why we will all sing, "To him who sits on the throne and to the Lamb be blessing and honor and glory and might forever and ever!" (Rev. 5:13).

But grumbling is the accent of hell's language, because it's how a creature's pride responds to the Creator's decision to do or to allow something that the creature does not desire. Grumbling scorns God because it elevates our desires and judgments above his.

That's why the world is so filled with grumbling. It's ruled by the prince of the power of the air (Eph. 2:2), and its citizens speak the official language.

Do All Things without Grumbling

And that's why Paul tells us to "do all things without grumbling" (Phil. 2:14). The children of God should not speak with the accent of hell.

Rather, our speech should always be gracious (Col. 4:6); it should have the accent of heaven. Those who have been forgiven so much (Luke 7:47) and promised so much (2 Pet. 1:4) should speak words that are always salted with gratitude (Eph. 5:20). That's one way we "shine as lights in the world" (Phil. 2:15). Gospel gratitude is a foreign language here. We are citizens of a better country (Heb. 11:16).

Doing *all things* without grumbling is humanly impossible. But thankfully not with God (Mark 10:27). What it requires is getting our eyes off ourselves and onto Jesus (Heb. 12:2) and all God promises to be for us in him. It requires *seeing* grace. *Being* different comes from *seeing* differently.

Here's the Bible logic that provides the escape from the temptation to grumble (1 Cor. 10:13): "*All things* work together for [my] good" (Rom. 8:28), and "I can do *all things* through him who strengthens me" (Phil. 4:13), so therefore I can "do *all things* without grumbling" (Phil. 2:14).

Yes, it's hard. It's a fight. God told us it would be that way (1 Tim. 6:12). But we will grow in the gracious habit of cultivating gratitude through the rigorous exercise of constant practice (Heb. 5:14) of seeing grace.

Lord, help us speak more in the accent of heaven!

Prone to grumbling, Lord, I feel it,
Prone to scorn the God I love;
Here's my eye, O take and peel it
Till I see the grace above.

Then "the words of my mouth and the meditation of my heart [will] be acceptable in your sight, O Lord, my rock and my redeemer" (Ps. 19:14).

Give thanks in all circumstances; for this is
the will of God in Christ Jesus for you.

1 THESSALONIANS 5:18

8

HOW CAN WE GIVE THANKS IN ALL CIRCUMSTANCES?

IN THE PREVIOUS CHAPTER, I described grumbling as the accent of hell and gratitude as the accent of heaven. In this chapter, let's take a longer look at gratitude.

More specifically, how is it possible to obey 1 Thessalonians 5:18 and "give thanks in all circumstances," especially if our circumstances are horrible? What fuels thanksgiving when life seems to be one discouragement, disappointment, disease, disaster, and death after another?

There is only one way. And Jesus both shows the way and *is* the way (John 14:6).

Eucharisteo: Thanks in the Face of Horror

The best place to see Jesus showing us the way is in the upper room, where "he took bread, and when he had given thanks, he broke it and gave it to them, saying, 'This is my body, which is given for you. Do this in remembrance of me'" (Luke 22:19). The Greek word for "thanks" in this verse is *eucharisteo*. Ann Voskamp beautifully unpacks its meaning:

The root word of *eucharisteo* is *charis* meaning "grace." Jesus took the bread and saw it as grace and gave thanks. He took the bread and knew it to be gift and gave thanks. *Eucharisteo*, thanksgiving, envelopes the Greek word for grace, *charis*. But it also holds its derivative, the Greek word *chara*, meaning "joy." Charis. Grace. *Eucharisteo*. Thanksgiving. *Chara*. Joy.[8]

Now, let's ponder for a moment about what Jesus's *eucharisteo* meant:

> Thank you, Father, that my body, symbolized by this bread, is about to be brutally broken, and I am about to be (momentarily) damned by your wrath (Isa. 53:10) so that you will receive supreme glory in being able to forgive undeserving sinners (Phil. 2:11), and I will share eternally full joy (John 15:11; Ps. 16:11) with hundreds of millions of forgiven sinners made righteous through my sacrifice (Isa. 53:11).

Jesus's thanks was not based on his present circumstances. He was about to endure the worst possible horror. He felt thankful to the Father for the grace and glory that was coming because of the cross, and this gave him joy. *Eucharisteo*.

---

8   Glynn Young, "Don't Worry, Be Thankful: *Eucharisteo* with Ann Voskamp," *The High Calling* website, November 21, 2014, accessed September 26, 2015, http://www.thehighcalling.org/articles/essay/dont-worry-be-thankful-eucharisteo-ann-voskamp#.Uo4zc6Wb-zg.

Future Joy Fuels Your Thankful Endurance

Jesus's *eucharisteo* was fueled by his belief in future grace.[9] That's what the author of Hebrews meant when he wrote that "Jesus, the founder and perfecter of our faith . . . for the joy that was set before him endured the cross, despising the shame, and is seated at the right hand of the throne of God" (Heb. 12:2).

Jesus's eyes were on his future joy—the joy set before him. He got through the cross by focusing not on the cross but on the promised joy that would result from it.

That's where God wants your eyes: on the future joy he has promised you.

---

9 John Piper has written an excellent book titled *Future Grace: The Purifying Power of the Promises of God*, rev. ed. (Colorado Springs: Multnomah, 2012). For a helpful, very brief explanation, see "Rebuilding Some Basics of Bethlehem: The Purifying Power of Living by Faith in Future Grace," *Desiring God* website, October 8, 2009, accessed September 29, 2015, http://www.desiringgod.org/articles/rebuilding-some-basics-of-bethlehem-the-purifying-power-of-living-by-faith-in-future grace. Here's an excerpt:

> [God's] grace is past and it is future. It is ever cascading over the infinitesimal waterfall of the present from the inexhaustible river of grace coming to us from the future into the ever-increasing reservoir of grace in the past. In the next five minutes, you will receive sustaining grace flowing to you from the future, and you will accumulate another five minutes' worth of grace in the reservoir of the past.
>
> The proper response to grace you experienced in the past is *gratitude*, and the proper response to grace promised to you in the future is *faith*. We are *thankful* for past grace, and we are *confident* in future grace.

What You Have to Look Forward To

And what is your future joy? The very best possible future you could ever imagine—if you will believe it.

- You will have the free gift of complete forgiveness of all your sins, extending into eternity (Rom. 6:23).
- You will never have to merit your justification by keeping the law (Gal. 2:16).
- You will have all your real needs provided while on earth (Phil. 4:19).
- You will receive all the grace you need at all times so that you will abound in every good work God has for you (2 Cor. 9:8).
- God will complete the good work he began in you (Phil. 1:6).
- You will be raised from the dead and never, ever die again (1 Cor. 15:52–53).
- That means someday soon you will see Jesus, be with him (2 Cor. 5:8), and be like him (1 John 3:2).
- In that day you will know for the first time full, unpolluted joy (Ps. 16:11).
- You will be completely free from all corruption (Rom. 8:21).
- You will have God forever (1 Pet. 3:18) as your exceeding joy (Ps. 43:4).

And that's just a small sampling! The joy set before you is the same joy Jesus had set before him, because you are an heir of the kingdom with him (Rom. 8:17).

Look to the Joy Set Before You

So right now you have trouble. That's okay. Jesus said that you would (John 16:33). And Jesus really understands (Heb. 4:15).

In fact, the trouble that you endure has a purpose: in it you are displaying the reality of Jesus to the world in a unique way. The kingdom of God is most clearly shown on earth when Christians gratefully suffer present trouble because they see a future weight of glory coming that makes everything this world throws at them as "light and momentary afflictions" in comparison (2 Cor. 4:17).

So how can you give thanks in all circumstances? There's only one way: Jesus's way. Look to the joy set before you. Look to the joy!

If the future joy Jesus promises is real, and you believe him, there is no circumstance that can steal your thanksgiving.

If you abide in me, and my words abide in you, ask whatever you wish, and it will be done for you.

JOHN 15:7

9

THE UNEXPECTED ANSWERS OF GOD

IN JOHN 16:23-24 JESUS makes a stunning, sweeping, glorious promise to us:

> In that day you will ask nothing of me. Tru-
> ly, truly, I say to you, whatever you ask of the
> Father in my name, he will give it to you. Until
> now you have asked nothing in my name. Ask,
> and you will receive, that your joy may be full.

So we ask the Father for things we long for because we want the full joy he offers us. And we don't ask for trivial or fleshly things because we know what the apostle James says: "You ask and do not receive, because you ask wrongly, to spend it on your passions" (James 4:3). No, we pray for greater faith, love, holiness, wisdom, discernment, experience of God's grace, boldness, joy in God, and less satisfaction with worldly things.

Unexpected Answers

Such longings and prayers are sincere, and God loves them and loves to answer them. But we do not know ourselves very well, nor the depth or pervasiveness of our sin, nor what it really requires of us in order to receive what we ask for. We can't help but have unreal, romantic imaginations and expectations about what God's answers to our prayers will be.

Therefore, we are often unprepared for the answers we receive from God. His answers frequently do not look at first like answers. They look like problems. They look like trouble. They look like loss, disappointment, affliction, conflict, sorrow, and increased selfishness. They cause deep soul wrestling and expose sins and doubts and fears. They are not what we expect, and we often do not see how they correspond to our prayers.

What Should We Expect?

If we ask God for greater, deeper love for him, what should we expect to receive? Answers that give us a greater awareness of our deep and pervasive sinful depravity, because those who are forgiven much, love much, but those who are forgiven little, love little (Luke 7:47).

If we ask God to help us love our neighbors as ourselves (Mark 12:31), what should we expect to receive? Answers that force us to give unplanned attention to a neighbor, perhaps an unexpected neighbor (Luke 10:29), which feel inconvenient and irritating.

If we ask for God's nearness because we believe that it is good for us to be near God (Ps. 73:28), what should we expect to receive? Answers that break our hearts, for God is near to the brokenhearted (Ps. 34:18).

If we ask God to make us living sacrifices (Rom. 12:2), what should we expect to receive? Answers that break and humble our hearts, because the sacrifices of God are a broken spirit (Ps. 51:17).

If we ask God for a deeper experience of his grace, what should we expect to receive? Answers that oppose our pride and humble our hearts (James 4:6).

If we ask God for his kingdom to come (Matt. 6:10) in our own lives and in the world around us, what should we expect to receive? Answers that reveal our deep spiritual poverty, because the kingdom is given to the poor in spirit (Matt. 5:3).

If we ask God to satisfy us with himself so that we aren't so easily satisfied by the world's mud puddles, what should we expect to receive? Answers that cause us to be increasingly aware of the evil and suffering and injustices of the world, because those who hunger and thirst for righteousness will be satisfied (Matt. 5:6).

If we ask God for greater wisdom and discernment, what should we expect to receive? A steady stream of mind-bending, confusing answers that are difficult to understand and work through, because our powers of discernment are trained by constant practice to distinguish good from evil (Heb. 5:14).

If we ask God to "increase our faith" (Luke 17:5), what should we expect to receive? Repeatedly being placed in situations where we discover that our perceptions are not trustworthy so that we are forced to trust Christ's promises, "for we walk by faith, not by sight" (2 Cor. 5:7).

If we ask God to help us "walk in a manner worthy of the Lord" (Col. 1:10), what should we expect to receive? Answers that require more humility, gentleness, patience, and bearing with one another in love (Eph. 4:2) than we thought possible and might result in destitution, affliction, and mistreatment, like many saints throughout history "of whom the world was not worthy" (Heb. 11:38).

If we ask God to help us stop serving money so that we can serve him more wholeheartedly, what should we expect to receive? An uncomfortable amount of opportunities to give money away, expenses that deplete reserves we've been stashing away, maybe even a job loss—answers that push us to despise (ignore, turn away from, release) money and cling to God (Luke 16:13).

If we ask for our joy to be made more full (John 16:24), to experience more happiness in God, what should we expect to receive? Answers that cause us to find earthly joys we once thought gain to become empty, hollow, and loss and to push us to search for the surpassing value of knowing Christ Jesus and find him as gain above all else (Phil. 3:8).

Expect the Unexpected

When God begins to answer our prayers, we often find his answers disorienting. Circumstances might take unexpected courses, health might deteriorate, painful relational dynamics might develop, financial difficulties might occur, and spiritual and emotional struggles might emerge that seem unconnected to our prayers, and we can feel like we're digressing from not progressing toward the sanctification we desire. We cry out in painful confusion and exasperation (Ps. 13:1; Job 30:20), when what's really happening is that God is answering our prayers. We just expected the answer to look and feel different.

This being true, we might be tempted to not even ask God for such things. I mean, who wants unpleasant answers to prayers for joy?

Don't be deceived into this shortsighted thinking. Remember Jesus's promise: "Ask, and you will receive, that your joy may be full" (John 16:24). If the path to full joy is sometimes hard, and Jesus tells us it is (John 16:33; Matt. 7:14), that is no reason not to take it! What do you want? Low, shallow, thin joys? No! Go for full joy. And remember what the writer of Hebrews tells us:

> For the moment all discipline seems painful rather than pleasant, but later it yields the peaceful fruit of righteousness to those who have been trained by it. (Heb. 12:11)

When it comes to God answering our prayers, expect the unexpected. Most of the greatest gifts and deepest joys that God gives us come wrapped in painful packages.

The LORD gave, and the LORD has taken away; blessed be the name of the LORD.

JOB 1:21

10

WHAT GOD GIVES WHEN HE TAKES AWAY

WHAT WE REALLY LOVE and trust aren't truly seen until we are tested by loss.

This is essentially the point that Satan made when talking to God about Job. In that odd scene in the first chapter of Job, when Satan presented himself before God, God said to him, "Have you considered my servant Job, that there is none like him on the earth, a blameless and upright man, who fears God and turns away from evil?" (Job 1:8).

Satan's response was,

> Does Job fear God for no reason? Have you not put a hedge around him and his house and all that he has, on every side? You have blessed the work of his hands, and his possessions have increased in the land. But stretch out your hand and touch all that he has, and he will curse you to your face. (Job 1:9–11)

Yeah, God, of course Job "fears" you when his life is full of blessings. But take away the blessings, and his trust will turn to cursing.

Note the irony here. In this manipulative moment, Satan inadvertently pointed out the core error of pros-

perity theology: prosperity obscures rather than reveals
how much fallen humans love God. "Blessings" easily
turn into curses as sinners subtly (or not so subtly)
come to love and trust the blessings more than the
bless-er.

Satan knew this by experience. He was so confident
that Job would curse God if the blessings were removed
because he had seen it occur thousands and thousands
of times in others.

Satan knew that the taking away more than the giving would reveal the truth—what Job really trusted and
loved. So did God. So God gave Satan permission to take
away Job's children, wealth, health, and reputation—all
that most men place their hope in during life.

And the result?

> Then Job arose and tore his robe and shaved
> his head and fell on the ground and worshiped.
> And he said, "Naked I came from my mother's
> womb, and naked shall I return. The LORD gave,
> and the LORD has taken away; blessed be the
> name of the LORD." (Job 1:20–21)

Satan was proven wrong about Job.

When You Know You Love Her

But Satan wasn't wrong about the concealing power of
prosperity and the revealing power of loss. Even the
world sometimes catches glimpses of this principle, as
the band Passenger captures in the song "Let Her Go":

Well you only need the light when it's burning
low;
Only miss the sun when it starts to snow;
Only know you love her when you let her go.

Only know you've been high when you're feeling
low;
Only hate the road when you're missin' home;
Only know you love her when you let her go.[10]

You "only know you love her when you let her go."
Having conceals love; loss reveals love.

Satan gets no pleasure out of humans enjoying real
pleasure. He would prefer to kill, maim, steal, destroy,
and deprive, if doing so doesn't push someone toward
faith in God (John 10:10).

But he also knows that a consistently effective tool
to weaken, impede, and disease the church is to let her
prosper. Prosperity has a greater tendency to conceal
idolatry and false faith. So, like he tried with Jesus, Satan sometimes will offer us the world (Luke 4:5–7). He
would rather us be faithlessly prosperous than afflicted
and faithful.

Loss for the Sake of the True Prosperity Gospel

But Jesus wants us to embrace the true prosperity gospel. He wants us to have real "treasure in heaven" (Mark

---

10 Mike Rosenberg, "Let Her Go," from the album *All the Little Lights*,
performed by Passenger. Produced by Mike Rosenberg and Chris
Vallejo. Nettwerk, Embassy of Music, Inertia Pty. Limited, 2012.

10:21), the gift of "pleasures forevermore" (Ps. 16:11). So when Jesus calls us, he often asks us to leave homes, land, family, and vocations for his sake and the gospel's (Mark 10:29). He requires us to deny ourselves and take up our cross (Matt. 16:24). Because, like Paul described, when for Christ's sake we are willing to abandon those things that the world considers the only gain worth having, it shows that Christ is truly gain to us (Phil. 3:8).

It is also why, when God disciplines us (Heb. 12:5–6) to conform us to the image of his Son (Rom. 8:29), he will, like Job, take away earthly things that are precious to us. The affections of our hearts, both sinful and righteous, that were more concealed in the having are more revealed in the losing. The sin that is revealed he seeks to mortify; the righteousness of faith that is revealed he seeks to display for us and for the watching world.

Testing Is More Than Just for Us

Yes, our testing is more than just for us. We must remember that, like Job's experience, there is often more going on in our experience than meets our eyes.

Job didn't know when the calamities hit that God was putting Satan to shame. Peter and the disciples wouldn't have known Satan's involvement in their temptations during the Passion week had Jesus not told them (Luke 22:31). Likewise, we often aren't aware of the full cosmic struggle in which we are involved. But these texts (and others) remind us that this struggle is real and that we should be careful about jumping to conclusions based on our perceptions alone.

God Takes Away for Our Joy

The crucial thing for us to remember is that all that God does for us as his children is for our good. He is blessed in both the giving and the taking away because both are for the sake of our joy.

Often it is in the taking away that our true love and trust are revealed, which is a great mercy to us and usually for others. And often, in this age, the most valuable, most satisfying, most beneficial, longest-lasting gifts we receive and pass along to others end up coming through the experiences of our losses.

My grace is sufficient for you, for my power is made perfect in weakness.

2 CORINTHIANS 12:9

11

THE PRICELESS GRACE OF PRESSURE

PRESSURE IS ONE OF the more resented of God's graces.

I'm not wired to appreciate pressure. But I am wired to need it. I find that when the pressure is on, I often wish it were off. But I also find that when the pressure is off, I tend to waste more time. I have a persistent misconception that I am more creative when the pressure is off. But, while that may be true for a few things, as a general rule it has not been my actual experience. Necessity tends to produce resourcefulness. Deadlines tend to induce creativity. Leisure tends to induce indulgence and procrastination.

Not everyone is wired the same way. There are more driven temperaments that have an inner compulsion to get lots of things done no matter if there are deadlines or not. Bless them. But in my observation, those temperaments are rare. Most of us will tend to do less if less is required.

It is, no doubt, an effect of the curse, a manifestation of the pathological selfishness that is part of our fallen nature. But that being the case, the discomfort of pressure to prod us forward is a gift to be desired, not an annoyance to be avoided.

Biblical Pressure

Read the Bible and you'll find that, post-fall, it is one
story after another of pressurized saints. Noah, Abraham, Moses, Joshua, Ruth, Naomi, David, Daniel, Ezra,
Nehemiah, Jesus's disciples, and the apostles all dealt
with significant pressure. Paul felt a daily pressure of
concern for all the churches that kept him praying
without ceasing (2 Cor. 11:28; 1 Thess. 5:17). The press of
adversity and affliction called for the exercising of faith,
the one thing without which we will never please God
(Heb. 11:6).

When God chooses his servants, he tends to give
them an oversized workload. Yes, God works for those
who wait for him (Isa. 64:4), but you'll note that waiting
on God is rarely experienced as a leisure activity. It typi-
cally involves being placed in an overwhelming situation
that requires a steeling of the nerves of faith to wait.
Yes, we are to serve in the strength that God supplies (1
Pet. 4:11), but that serving can still push us beyond what
we think we can handle to show that it's God's gracious
supply, not our own strength, that is sufficient (2 Cor.
12:9) and to show that we hope in the God who raises
the dead (2 Cor. 1:8–9).

He "knows our frame; he remembers that we are
dust" (Ps. 103:14). And so he gives us some seasons of
green pastures and still waters (Ps. 23:2). But rarely as
many as we would wish. And often not when we think
we need it. God knows far better than we do when
we really need refreshment and when we need to be
pushed. It is precisely because God knows our frame,
and what kind of dust we really are, that he mercifully

doesn't relent the pressure—because when the pressure is off, we have a tendency to forget our need for God (1 Sam. 12:9; Rev. 3:17). Our proneness to wander is curbed by the priceless grace of pressure.

An Answer to Our Prayer for "More"

I have noticed a pattern that when I ask God for more— to know more of his grace, to trust his promises more than my perceptions, for a deeper understanding of his Word, for greater discernment and wisdom, for more love for others, for more self-control, for more of his Holy Spirit's empowerment—what I receive is more pressure. And frequently the kind of pressure I receive is often not what I thought I was asking for, so I am at first confused and sometimes sinfully frustrated. My conception (my imagination) of what "more" I needed was different from God's.

For example, I'm distractible. I probably fall somewhere on the spectrum of ADHD. Therefore, I can intuitively assume that life would be better if I had fewer demands. But that's not the Lord's assessment. Instead, he has assigned me to lead a family of seven, help lead an internet ministry, pastor bi-vocationally in my local church, be a legal guardian for my disabled sister, and try to manage all the things that come with just normal life and my own spiritual struggles.

My labors are not heroic. I know others who do far more. But I have prayed often about whether God wants me to do less, and he keeps directing me to the same answer Paul received about his thorn (though I blush at even alluding to such a comparison): "My grace is sufficient for you, for my power is made perfect in weakness" (2 Cor. 12:9).

Over the years, I have found this to be true. I often feel pressed and at times anxious. And yet there has always been enough grace. In fact, the grace is often the very pressure I am tempted to resent. Distractibility doesn't improve with less pressure; it just runs freer. Pressure forces focus and helps me to make the most of my time (Eph. 5:16).

Pray for More!

If knowing that praying for more grace may result in more pressure, we may be tempted not to ask for more. When we feel this way, we must repent. Because we do not know as we ought to know (1 Cor. 8:2). No good thing will God withhold from those who walk uprightly (Ps. 84:11). Only a fool prefers evil over good, or even less good over more good. We don't want to be fools.

Jesus promises that if we ask in faith and in his name, the Father will grant what we ask for our joy (John 16:24). Yes, our joy! God only gives us the priceless grace of pressure so that we will share his holiness, bear the peaceful fruit of righteousness (Heb. 12:10–11), exercise love for others (1 John 4:7), and put their needs before ours (Phil. 2:3–4), and to push us toward himself—our exceeding joy (Ps. 43:4).

So let's pray earnestly for more of whatever God wishes to give us. Let us boldly pray "whatever-it-takes prayers" and take whatever he gives us. And if he graciously answers us with more pressure than we expected, let us not resent it but recognize it as a gift to help us strive to enter the rest that is coming (Heb. 4:11).

*For the gate is narrow and the way is hard that
leads to life, and those who find it are few.*

MATTHEW 7:14

12

THE WAY IS HARD, BUT HE IS STRONG

"THE WAY IS HARD," Jesus said (Matt. 7:14).

In our early days we thought we knew what "hard" meant. Hard would be rigorous, demanding, exhausting. Jesus said the way would be hard, and with James and John we replied (if not in words, then in unspoken presumption), "We are able" (Matt. 20:22).

But like James and John, we didn't really understand what we were getting into. Like green recruits, we thought we understood what war was like. War is hard. War is hell. Especially when you war with hell.

But we didn't really understand hell's warfare until we really began to engage it. Then hell began to break loose, and we discovered that the chaos of war is far different experienced than studied.

Devils know no chivalry. They are cruel and conceal their cruelty in the Trojan horses of pleasure and comfort, "wisdom" and "security," flattery and shame. Theirs is guerilla warfare and espionage. Theirs is psychological warfare and seduction. Theirs is biological warfare and blackmail.

Hell's Primary Objective

Hell's primary objective is to destroy faith in God. All of its elaborate strategies and all of its diabolical energies are focused on one thing: breaking the power of the word of the Lord by undermining our trust in it. The universe was created and is upheld by the Word of God (John 1:3; Heb. 1:3), so hell must break the power of the Word of God if it wants to win.

Therefore, we find ourselves fighting an enemy that constantly seeks to alter our perception of reality. That is why this fight is such a surreal and sometimes horrific experience.

Hell wages a war of distortion. It seeks to make the most destructive things look tantalizingly desirable. It seeks to make the most wonderful things look unbearably boring. It seeks to make the most trustworthy things look unreliable. It seeks to make the one true fountain of joy look like a dry well, and a broken cistern look like a spring of refreshment. Hell makes even hell look entertaining.

Hell wages a war of disorientation. Through temptation, condemnation, intimidation, discouragement, disappointment, doubt, illness, weakness, weariness, and appeals to our pride and shame, the spiritual powers of evil seek to keep us off-balanced, confused, and turned around. For if we lose our focus on the truth, we lose our confidence and may lose our faith.

Hell wages a war of suspicion. One of the most painful things in this spiritual war is hell's infiltration into our relationships. It seeks to corrupt the currency of trust in which they trade. Marriages break, families fracture, friendships rupture, churches split, and movements derail as sin infects and seeds of suspicion are sowed and fertilized. And in the fray we easily lose track

of who the enemy is and end up fighting against flesh
and blood.

That Word above All Earthly Powers

Jesus was right: The way is hard—far harder than we
expected.

But Jesus was right about something else: "The gates
of hell will not prevail" (Matt. 16:18). The way is hard,
but the way is sure. For the Way (John 14:6) is the Word
(John 1:1).

And the Word is impenetrably strong.

All the brutal forces of hell, with all the distortion it
can conjure, disorientation it can cause, and suspicion it
can sow, simply cannot break the Word of God. Martin
Luther was right about the Devil: "one little word shall
fell him." O, but that Word turns out not to be so little.
For that Word is God himself (John 1:1).

And the Word came to destroy the works of the
Devil (1 John 3:8).

O, the paradox! The Word of God destroyed the
works of the Devil by being broken. Yes, all hell broke
loose upon the Word of God from Gethsemane to Calva-
ry, and the Word was broken. But it was not broken in
the way that hell tried to break it. Hell tried to compro-
mise the Word, but the Word held fast by being broken.
For in being broken, the Word of God kept unbroken
the word of God, the great covenant, and cosmic justice
was upheld as Christ became both "just and the justifier
of the one who has faith in Jesus" (Rom. 3:26).

That Word stands above all earthly powers and
smashes against the gates of hell.

The way may be hard for us. But the Way will be hell for hell.

The key to our clarity in the face of hell's distortion, our focus in the face of hell's disorientation, and our persevering, longsuffering love in the face of hell's suspicion is to listen to the Word of God by soaking in the words of God in the Bible. The Word is our refuge (Ps. 18:30), the Word is our peace (Acts 10:36; Phil. 4:7), and the Word is our weapon (Eph. 6:17).

We must remember that hell is after one thing: our faith. And we must remember that we will overcome hell by one thing: our faith (1 John 5:4). Jesus summarized our one and supreme defense against hell in this statement: "Believe in God; believe also in me" (John 14:1).

Therefore, today:

> Be sober-minded; be watchful. Your adversary the devil prowls around like a roaring lion, seeking someone to devour. Resist him, firm in your faith, knowing that the same kinds of suffering are being experienced by your brotherhood throughout the world. And after you have suffered a little while, the God of all grace, who has called you to his eternal glory in Christ, will himself restore, confirm, strengthen, and establish you. (1 Pet. 5:8–10)

We destroy arguments and every lofty opinion raised against the knowledge of God, and take every thought captive to obey Christ.

2 CORINTHIANS 10:5

13

WHERE SATAN WILL ATTACK YOU TODAY

YOU WONDER WHY IT'S so hard to find some peace of mind? Well, peace is hard to come by when you live in a war zone. And like it or not, you are in a war—a very serious one. This war is cosmic in its proportions. It involves God, humans, angels, demons, principalities, powers, nations, and antichrists.

And do you know where the front of the battle is? It's in your head.

We Destroy Arguments

Here is how Paul describes it in 2 Corinthians 10:3–5:

> For though we walk in the flesh, we are not waging war according to the flesh. For the weapons of our warfare are not of the flesh but have divine power to destroy strongholds. *We destroy arguments* and every lofty opinion raised against the knowledge of God, and take every thought captive to obey Christ.

What are the satanic strongholds that spiritually imprison people, the strongholds that we seek to destroy? Arguments and opinions. Where is the battle raging? In our thoughts.

Arguments are not merely strongholds; they are weapons of mass destruction. Adam and Eve (and all of us with them) fell because of an argument. They believed the Serpent's argument and stopped believing God.

That is the deadly essence of sin: not believing God. To not believe God is to ally with Satan, whom Jesus said is "a murderer from the beginning, and has nothing to do with the truth . . . for he is a liar and the father of lies" (John 8:44).

You don't want Satan as an ally. He's treacherous. He's out to murder you with lies.

Watch Your Emotions

Watch your emotions. They are signals of arguments. Your emotions, which can land on you like vague impressions or moods, are usually responses to an argument. Moods don't come out of nowhere. When we are angry, discouraged, depressed, anxious, self-pitying, fearful, or irritable, it is likely because we are believing something very specific.

To battle sin is to battle unbelief—or destroy arguments. And in order to battle unbelief effectively, we must press doubts and temptations into specific arguments. What specifically is being asserted or promised to us? Only then can we destroy the enemy's false arguments with true ones.

The Victory That Overcomes the World

The victory that overcomes the world is our faith (1 John 5:4). This is precisely why the Devil does not want us to think clearly about sin. He wants to keep things vague so he can imprison or disarm us. But Jesus wants us to think clearly. He wants us to know the truth because the truth brings freedom:

> If you abide in my word, you are truly my disciples, and you will know the truth and the truth will set you free. (John 8:31–32)

As freedom fighters we must fight against "unbelieving hearts" by exhorting one another every day (Heb. 3:12–13) to live in the freedom—and peace (John 16:33)—of the truth.

Because our most important battles are won and lost with arguments.

Therefore, preparing your minds for action, and being sober-minded, set your hope fully on the grace that will be brought to you at the revelation of Jesus Christ.

1 PETER 1:13

14

YOUR EMOTIONS ARE A GAUGE, NOT A GUIDE

YOUR REST IS COMING. Sooner than you know, you will receive your "imperishable, undefiled, and unfading inheritance" (1 Pet. 1:4). And when it comes you will understand why your faith was more precious than gold (1 Pet. 1:7). This is where Peter wants your hope to fully rest.

But today is a time for war, not peace. It's a time for faith, not sight. It's a time of grievous trials that test the genuineness of your faith (1 Pet. 1:6–7). So it's a time to prepare for the action of battle, to keep sober.

Your battle today will not be against "flesh and blood" but the deceitful forces of evil (Eph. 6:12) and the deceitfulness of indwelling sin (Heb. 3:13). And these two forces are going to try to use your emotions against you. So it might be helpful, by way of preparation, to remember the purpose of emotions so you can fight more effectively and know when to counter them.

God designed your emotions to be gauges, not guides. They're meant to report to you, not rule you. The pattern of your emotions (not every caffeine-induced or sleep-deprived one!) will give you a reading on where your hope is, because they are wired into what you believe and value—and how much.

That's why emotions such as delight (Ps. 37:4), affection (Rom. 12:10), fear (Luke 12:5), anger (Ps. 37:8), and joy (Ps. 5:11) are so important in the Bible. They reveal what your heart loves, trusts, and fears. At Desiring God we like to say, "Pleasure is the measure of your treasure," because the emotion of pleasure is a gauge that tells you what you love.

But because our emotions are wired into our fallen nature as well as into our regenerated nature, sin and Satan have access to them and will use them to try to manipulate us to act faithlessly. That's why our emotional responses to temptation can seem like imperatives (you must do) rather than indicatives (here's what you're being told). Just remember, that's deceit.

Emotions aren't imperatives; they're not your boss. They're indicatives; they're reports. That's why Paul wrote, "Let not sin therefore reign in your mortal body, to make you obey its passions" (Rom. 6:12).

So get ready. "Be sober-minded; be watchful. Your adversary the devil prowls around like a roaring lion, seeking someone to devour" (1 Pet. 5:8). He will make promises to and threats against you. He will likely tap into your weak areas of unbelief, and you may find your emotions surging in the wrong direction.

When that happens don't be overly impressed. And remember that your emotions are gauges, not guides. Let them tell you where the attack is being made so you can fight it with the right promises. And go to a trusted friend for prayer, perspective, and counsel if you need to.

And remember that this "light momentary affliction is preparing for [you] an eternal weight of glory beyond all comparison" (2 Cor. 4:17), and very soon it's going to be over. And God, your great reward, will be all the inheritance you will ever want forever.

Set your hope fully on that.

For with you is the fountain of life; in your light do we see light.

PSALM 36:9

15

SIX EXTRAORDINARY BENEFITS OF ORDINARY DAILY DEVOTIONS

OUR PRIVATE DEVOTIONS AREN'T magic. We know that.

But still, we can be tempted to think that if we just figure out the secret formula—the right mixture of Bible meditation and prayer—we will experience euphoric moments of rapturous communion with the Lord. And if that doesn't happen, our formula must be wrong.

The danger of this misconception is that it can produce chronic disappointment and discouragement. Cynicism sets in, and we give up or whip through them to alleviate guilt that results when devotions don't seem to work for us.

Our longing for intimate communion with God is God-given. It's a good thing to desire, ask for, and pursue. The Spirit does give us wonderful occasional tastes. And this longing will be satisfied to overflowing someday (Ps. 16:11).

But God has other purposes for us in the discipline of daily Bible meditation and prayer. Here are a few:

1. **Soul Exercise** (1 Cor. 9:24; Rom. 15:4): We exercise our bodies to increase strength and endurance, promote general health, and keep unnecessary weight off. Devotions are like exercise for our souls. They force our attention off of self-indulgent distractions and pursuits and on to God's purposes and promises. If we neglect this exercise, our souls will go to pot.

2. **Soul Shaping** (Rom. 12:2): The body will generally take the shape of how we exercise it. Running shapes one way, weight training shapes another way. The same is true for the soul. It will conform to how we exercise (or don't exercise) it. This is why changing your exercise routine can be helpful. Read through the Bible one year, camp in a book and memorize it another year, take a few months to meditate on and pray through texts related to an area of special concern, etc.

3. **Bible Copiousness** (Ps. 119:11, 97; Prov. 23:12): A thorough, repeated, soaking in the Bible over the course of years increases our overall biblical knowledge, providing fuel for the fire of worship and increasing our ability to draw from all parts of the Bible in applying God's wisdom to life.

4. **Fight Training** (Eph. 6:10–17): Marines undergo rigorous training in order to so ingrain their weapons knowledge that when suddenly faced with the chaos of combat they instinctively know

how to handle their weapons. Similarly, daily handling and using the sword of the Spirit (Eph. 6:17) makes us more skilled spiritual warriors.

5. **Sight Training** (2 Cor. 4:18; 5:7): Jesus really does want us to see and savor him. Savoring comes through seeing. But only the eyes of faith see him. "Blind faith" is a contradiction, at least biblically. Faith is not blind. Unbelief is blind (John 9:38–41). Faith is seeing a reality that physical eyes can't see and believing it (1 Pet. 1:8). And "faith comes from hearing, and hearing through the word of Christ" (Rom. 10:17). So if we're going to savor Jesus, we must see him in the word he speaks. Faith is a gift (Eph. 2.8). And like most of God's gifts, faith is intended to be cultivated. Daily devotions are an important way to train our faith-eyes to see the glory of Jesus in his word and training our emotions to respond to what our faith-eyes see. Keep looking for glory. Jesus will give you Emmaus moments (Luke 24:31–32).

6. **Delight Cultivation** (Ps. 37:3–4; 130:5; James 4:8): When a couple falls in love, there are hormonal fireworks. But when married they must cultivate delight in each other. It is the consistent, persistent, faithful, intentional, affectionate pursuit of one another during better and worse, richer and poorer, sickness and health that cultivates a capacity for delight in each other far deeper and richer than the fireworks phase. Similarly, de-

votions are one of the ways we cultivate delight in God. Many days they may seem mundane. But we will be surprised at the cumulative power they have to deepen our love for and awareness of him.

There are many more benefits. You could certainly add to this list. But the bottom line is this: Don't give up on daily devotions. Don't whip through them. Don't let them get crowded out by other demands.

Brick upon brick a building is built. Lesson upon lesson a degree is earned. Stroke upon stroke a painting is created. Your devotions may have seemed ordinary today, but God is making something extraordinary through it. Press on. Don't shortchange the process.

Let the word of Christ dwell in you richly, teaching and admonishing one another in all wisdom, singing psalms and hymns and spiritual songs, with thankfulness in your hearts to God.

COLOSSIANS 3:16

16

WHAT TO NEGLECT TO HAVE A RICH LIFE

COLOSSIANS 3:16 IS SO full of nourishment that there is no way to put the whole thing in our mouths at one time.

Today, let's just chew on the first word. "*Let* the word of Christ dwell in you richly."

Another way to say it is, don't stop the word of Christ from filling you to satisfaction. Or stop stopping it.

Here's the thing: we are frequently impoverished spiritually by our own not letting ourselves be rich. On our shelves or bed stands or in our tablets or computers is a bank vault of "true riches" (Luke 16:11). But the pawnshop trinkets of worldly words are deceptively attractive. We can even be on our way to spend our time (the currency of life) on the riches in the vault and end up spending it in the pawnshops along the way.

What Paul wants us to do is neglect things that make us poor and not neglect things that make us truly rich.

What to Neglect

If the words of the *Wall Street Journal* or *World* magazine or *Wired* magazine or David Brooks or David Letterman or David McCullough or John Mayer or John Steinbeck or John Calvin or Richard Dawkins or Richard Branson or Richard Baxter or Bono or Bach or blogs dwell in you more richly than the word of Christ, you're poor. You might be impressive at a dinner party or around a conference table or at small group. But you're poor. You're storing up dust.

You don't need to be in the know.

You don't need to be admired among the literati or respected in the guild. You don't need an impressive net worth. You don't need to be well traveled or well read. You don't need to be conversant in Portlandia or up on how many Twitter followers Taylor Swift has. You don't need to be politically articulate or current on the mommy blogs or the "young, restless, and Reformed" buzz. You don't need to see the movie. You don't need to read the novel. You don't need to look hip.

What Not to Neglect

But what you desperately need, more than anything else in the world, is the word of Christ dwelling in you richly.

No one speaks like Jesus Christ (John 7:46). He is the Word of God and the Word that is God (John 1:1). He is the Word of Life (1 John 1:1) and when he speaks, his word is living and active (Heb. 4:12), and he shows you the path of life (Ps. 16:11), and his words give you hope and joy and peace (Rom. 15:13).

Jesus is the one human being in all of history who speaks the very words of eternal life (John 6:68), and when you listen and believe his word, it becomes your life (Deut. 32:47), your food (John 6:51), your drink (John 4:14), and your light (Ps. 119:105).

Only Jesus has the words of life. Only him. That's why the Father pleads with us, "This is my beloved Son; listen to him" (Mark 9:7).

Everyone else's words are dust in the winds of time, and to chase them is to chase the wind (Eccles. 1:14). The precious few helpful, enlightening, even mortal life-preserving words are only of superficial help to us and in the end will blow away.

The only exceptions are those that help us (and others) listen to the word of Christ.

Let It!

Let the word of Christ dwell in you richly. Don't neglect it. Listen to his word. Soak in his word. Memorize his word. Eat and chew it slowly. Don't stop it from benefitting you.

Neglect the TV, blogs, social networks, video games, theaters, magazines, books, hobbies, chores, and pursuits that keep you from the Vault. Neglect the impoverishing pawnshop trinkets of words that will turn to dust in a day, a week, or a few years.

When it comes to life, time really is money. Time is how you spend your life. Don't waste it. Spend your best time buying "true riches."

I cry to you for help and you do not answer me; I stand,
and you only look at me. You have turned cruel to me.

JOB 30:20-21

17

WHEN GOD FEELS CRUEL

LET'S SAY YOU'RE PRAYING with a suffering friend who blurts out to God,

> I cry to you for help and you do not answer
> me; I stand, and you only look at me. You have
> turned cruel to me.

Would you wince? He just accused God of being cruel! Oh, my. Would you want to quickly pray a correction? "Lord, we're just so thankful that you are sovereign over everything and for the reality of Romans 8:28!"

Well, your prayer might be biblical, but so would be your friend's prayer. In fact, your hypothetical friend's prayer is actually in the Bible (Job 30:20–21) and came out of the mouth of the man God considered the most blameless and upright on earth in his lifetime (Job 1:8).

Thank God the Bible Is So Honest

Let's read Job's raw prayer again:

> I cry to you for help and you do not answer me;
>   I stand, and you only look at me.
> You have turned cruel to me.

Doesn't reading that anguished prayer of a godly man make you thankful? I love how honest the Bible is. The Bible just says it like it is, and sometimes just what it feels like. I love the fact that almost all the Bible's heroes are unvarnished, clay-footed sinners with warts we can all see. I love that sometimes they even wonder if God is just plain being cruel. Because that's what we short-sighted, weak, doubting, clay-footed, sinning stumblers wonder at times when we're suffering. It means there's hope for us when we feel overwhelmed and disappoint-ed and confused and disillusioned. The frankness of the Bible is a great mercy to us.

Our Feelings Are Unreliable Reporters

Can you identify with Job? You cry out to God in your affliction, and nothing seems to change. It's like God is just standing there watching you writhe. It feels cruel.

But this is not, in fact, what's really happening. That wasn't really the case for Job, and it's not really the case for us. What's true is that God is doing far more in our affliction than we know at the time.

For Job, he didn't know that he was putting Satan to shame by trusting in God despite his desolate confusion. He didn't know that his experience would encourage millions for millennia. He just knew that his pain felt unbearable at times, and it didn't seem like God was do-ing anything to help. And like Job, we don't know what mind-blowing designs God has in store for what may feel unbearable and appear cruel today.

But we do know this: God was answering Job when it seemed he wasn't. And God was remembering David when David cried, "Will you forget me forever?" (Ps. 13:1). And when Jesus cried, "My God, My God, why have you forsaken me?" (Matt. 27:46), God had turned his face away from our sin, only to raise his Son from the dead to undying, unsurpassed, and eternal glory.

These texts and Job's prayer and many others in the Bible help us remember that sometimes it feels like God's being cruel when he's really not. They remind us that we can't trust what it *feels* like God is doing; we can only trust what God *says* he is doing. We all know from a thousand experiences that our feelings are unreliable reporters.

Be Quick to Listen, Slow to Correct, and Take Heart

These texts also remind us that godly people sometimes feel and express these intense emotions. And often what they need from us in that moment is not an immediate remedial theological course. What they need is a fellow groaner who will sit in silence with them and, when it's helpful, point them to the empathetic saints of Scripture who felt similar things and found God faithful after all.

Your or your loved one's suffering may be inscrutable today. But in reality it is preparing for you or them "an eternal weight of glory beyond all comparison" (2 Cor. 4:17). Take heart and hold on. If God feels cruel today, you will discover someday that it was a pain-induced mirage and that he had graces planned for your joy beyond anything you ever dreamed possible.

"And after you have suffered a little while, the God of all grace, who has called you to his eternal glory in

Christ, will himself restore, confirm, strengthen, and establish you" (1 Pet. 5:10).

Come, let us go down and there confuse their language,
so that they may not understand one another's speech.

GENESIS 11:7

18

WHEN GOD MERCIFULLY RUINS OUR PLANS

IT IS A PRICELESS gift when someone shows you a gospel treasure hidden in plain sight in the Bible. A good friend did this for me when preaching an excellent sermon on the tower of Babel from Genesis 11. Here are a few insights I gleaned from him.

When Our Aim Is Our Name . . .

You know the Tower of Babel story. The ancient people living on the plain of Shinar said,

"Come, let us build ourselves a city and a tower with its top in the heavens, and let us make a name for ourselves, lest we be dispersed over the face of the whole earth" (Gen. 11:4).

The Mesopotamians had one aim: to make a name for themselves. God was not present in their aim. They were aiming at their own greatness.

And in these ancient *Babel*-onians we can see a picture of ourselves. Like them, we are sinners too often full of pride and selfish ambition, giving way too much thought to what others think about us and what our legacy will be. Like them, we too often have a ridicu-lous, exaggerated desire for our own glory and can put great effort into marshaling our resources and systems to achieve it.

. . . God Will Mercifully Mess Up Our Aim

But here's how God responded to the ziggurat of human pride: "And the LORD came down to see the city and the tower, which the children of man had built" (Gen. 11:5).

The fact that God "came down" to view what men had built puts us all in our place. As my friend eloquently said, "God always has to 'come down' to examine our anthill achievements built in the sidewalk cracks of his creation."

And so in his Trinitarian counsel, the Lord said,

> Behold, they are one people, and they have all one language, and this is only the beginning of what they will do. And nothing that they propose to do will now be impossible for them. Come, let us go down and there confuse their language, so that they may not understand one another's speech." So the LORD dispersed them from there over the face of all the earth, and they left off building the city. (Gen. 11:6–8)

Let us make no mistake. God was not feeling threatened in his supremacy by collective human ingenuity. Rather, what God knew, and what the city builders did not know, was the devastation that sin would wreak if human pride were allowed to progress unimpeded.

We, who now have the benefit of observing a few thousand years of recorded history, should know better than our ancient predecessors. The technologically accelerated twentieth century, and the thousands upon thousands of war dead we memorialize today, bear witness to how much evil can be unleashed when the best and brightest human minds put their heads together to build their Babels.

"There is a way that seems right to a man, but its end is the way to death" (Prov. 14:12).

So God confused Mesopotamians' language and scattered them. And it was a great mercy. As my friend put it, "It was the mercy of God for him to make their lives difficult, mess up their one great aim, and give them what they hoped wouldn't happen."

God's Gracious Purposes in Our Disorienting Disappointments

And God does the same kind of merciful confounding in our lives. And it is far more merciful than we know, certainly more merciful than it feels when we are confounded.

We often do not know what we are really building when we embark on our achievements. We often aren't aware of how deep, pervasive, and motivating our pride is. We often are blind to how much we cherish the glory of our name. But God knows. And in mercy he confounds us, impedes us, and humbles us. And it is all mercy. "God opposes the proud but gives grace to the humble" (1 Pet. 5:5). When it comes to his children, God gives us grace in the act of opposing our pride, because it makes us humble. For he knows that the more humble we are, the happier we are. The proud will be destroyed (Prov. 16:18), but the humble will dwell with God (Isa. 57:15).

The story of the tower of Babel contains a gospel treasure: even our disorienting disappointments and failures in making a name for ourselves have redemptive purposes. God loves us and knows what is best for us, and in mercy he will not allow any achievement that we pursue for our own glory to rob us of the surpassing worth of knowing Christ Jesus (Phil. 3:8).

There is no real gain in making our name known. That's Philippians 3:8 rubbish. The only real gain is Christ. So God mercifully thwarts our pride-fueled plans in order to make us truly happy.

I cry to you for help and you do not answer me; I stand, and you only look at me.

JOB 30:20

19

WHEN GOD SEEMS SILENT

GOD CAN BE MADDENINGLY hard to get. When God says that his ways are not our ways, he really means it (Isa. 55:8).

We have these encounters with him where he breaks into our lives with power and answers our prayers and wins our trust, and he waters the garden of our faith, making it lush and green.

And then there are these seasons when chaos careens with apparent carelessness through our lives and the world, leaving us shattered. Or an unrelenting darkness descends. Or an arid wind we don't even understand blows across our spiritual landscape, leaving the crust of our soul cracked and parched. And we cry to God in our confused anguish, but he just seems silent. He seems absent.

Singing to the Silence

That's why tears tend to flow when I listen to Andrew Peterson's song "The Silence of God." I know what he means:

> It's enough to drive a man crazy, it'll break a
> man's faith,

It's enough to make him wonder, if he's ever
been sane.
When he's bleating for comfort from Thy staff
and Thy rod
And the Heaven's only answer is the silence of
God.[11]

The same thing happens when I listen to Rich Mullins's
song "Hard to Get":

Do you remember when you lived down here
where we all scrape
To find the faith to ask for daily bread?
Did you forget about us after you had flown
away?
Well I memorized ev'ry word you said.
Still I'm so scared I'm holding my breath,
While you're up there just playing hard to get.[12]

All of God's saints, if allowed to live long enough, are
led into the lonely, disorienting, weary wilderness. And
while there, we lament. And since laments are often
better sung than said, it has always been the poets and
songwriters who help us most:

Job: "I cry to you for help and you do not answer me; I stand, and you only look at me." (Job
30:20)

---

11 Andrew Peterson, "The Silence of God," from the album *Love and
   Thunder*. Provident Music Distribution, 2003.
12 Rich Mullins, "Hard to Get," from the album *The Jesus Record*. Word
   Entertainment, 1998.

King David: "My God, my God, why have you forsaken me? Why are you so far from saving me, from the words of my groaning? O my God, I cry by day, but you do not answer, and by night, but I find no rest." (Ps. 22:1–2)

The Flat Earth and the Absent God

Atheists will tell us that the reason God seems silent is that he's absent. "No one's home at that address. Duh."

In the silent suffering seasons we can be tempted to believe it, until we step back and take a look and see that existence itself is not silent. It screams God (Rom. 1:20). As Parmenides said, and Maria (*The Sound of Music*) sang, "Nothing comes from nothing; nothing ever could."[13]

Believing atheism is like moderns believing in a flat earth. "From where I stand, it doesn't look like God is there." Right. And if you only trust your perceptions, the world looks flat. You know the world is round only because of authoritative scientific revelation and many corroborating testimonies.

What we experience as God's absence or distance or silence is phenomenological. It's how we perceive it. It's how at some point it looks and feels, but it isn't how it is. Just like we can experience the world as flat when we're walking on a huge spinning ball, we can experience God as absent or distant, when "in him we live and move and have our being" (Acts 17:28).

---

13 Richard Rogers, "Something Good," performed by Julie Andrews and Christopher Plummer. Williamson Music, 1964.

In reality God wasn't absent or silent or indifferent
at all toward Job or King David. It's just how it felt to
them at the time. Nor, in reality, was God silent toward Andrew Peterson or playing hard to get with Rich
Mullins. And when we feel forsaken by God, we are not
forsaken (Heb. 13:5). We are simply called to trust the
promise more than the perception.

Why the Silence?

But why does it need to feel that way? Why the per-
ceived silence? Why can it seem like God is playing hard
to get or like he's just standing there looking at us when
we cry to him for help?

I don't claim to understand all the mysteries of this
experience. No doubt we underestimate the effects of
remaining sin and our need for this discipline in order
to share God's holiness (Heb. 12:10). But I believe there
are clues for another purpose as well. I'll phrase them as
questions.

- Why is it that "absence makes the heart grow fond-
  er" but "familiarity breeds contempt"?
- Why is water so much more refreshing when we're
  really thirsty?
- Why am I almost never satisfied with what I have,
  but always longing for more?
- Why can the thought of being denied a desire for
  marriage or children or freedom or some other
  dream create in us a desperation we previously
  didn't have?

- Why do deprivation, adversity, scarcity, and suffering often produce the best character qualities in us, while prosperity, ease, and abundance often produce the worst?

Do you see it? There is a pattern in the design of deprivation: deprivation draws out desire. Absence heightens desire. And the more heightened the desire, the greater its satisfaction will be. It is the mourning who will know the joy of comfort (Matt. 5:4). It is the hungry and thirsty who will be satisfied (Matt. 5:6). Longing makes us ask, emptiness makes us seek, silence makes us knock (Luke 11:9).

Deprivation is in the design of this age. We live mainly in the age of anticipation, not gratification. We live in the dim-mirror age, not the face-to-face age (1 Cor. 13:12). The paradox is that what satisfies us most in this age is not what we receive, but what we are promised. The chase is better than the catch in this age because the catch we're designed to be satisfied with is in the age to come.

And so Frederick William Faber wrote in his poem "The Desire of God":

Yes, pine for thy God, fainting soul! ever pine;
    Oh languish mid all that life brings thee of mirth;

> Famished, thirsty, and restless—let such life be
> thine—
> For what sight is to heaven, desire is to
> earth.[14]

(Thank God for poets and songwriters!)

So you desire God and ask for more of him, and what do you get? Stuck in a desert feeling deserted. You feel disoriented and desperate. Don't despair. The silence, the absence, is phenomenological. It's how it feels; it's not how it is. You are not alone. God is with you (Ps. 23:4). And he is speaking all the time in the priceless gift of the objective Word so you don't need to rely on the subjective impressions of your fluctuating emotions.

If desire is to earth what sight is to heaven, then God answers our prayer with more desire. It's the desert that awakens and sustains desire. It's the desert that dries up our infatuation with worldliness. And it's the desert that draws us to the well of the world to come.

14 Frederick Faber, "Desire of God," Finest of Wheat Teaching Fellowship, accessed September 28, 2015, http://www.finestofthewheat.org/Poetry/Desire_Of_God.php.

For the moment all discipline seems painful rather than pleasant, but later it yields the peaceful fruit of righteousness to those who have been trained by it.

HEBREWS 12:11

20

WHEN IT FEELS LIKE GOD IS PUNISHING YOU

AS A CHRISTIAN, WHEN you experience a painful providence such as an illness or a rebellious child or a broken marriage or a financial hardship or a persecution, do you ever wonder if God is punishing you for some sin you committed?

If you do, there is some very good news from the letter to the Hebrews.

The original readers of this letter had been experiencing persecution and affliction for some time. They were tired, discouraged, and confused—why was God allowing such hardships? And some were battling doubt.

So after some doctrinal clarifications and firm exhortations, and a few sober warnings (so they could examine if their faith was real), the author of the letter brought home a very important point.

He wanted his readers to remember that the difficulty and pain they were experiencing was not God's punishment for their sins or weak faith. Chapters 7–10 beautifully explain that Jesus's sacrifice for sin was once—for all believers for all time (Heb. 10:14). No sacrifice of any kind for sin was ever needed again (Heb. 10:18).

He followed that up in chapter 11 with example after example of how the life of faith has always been difficult for saints.

And then he wrote the tender encouragement and exhortation of 12:5–6, where he quoted Proverbs 3:11–12:

> My son, do not regard lightly the discipline of the Lord,
> nor be weary when reproved by him.
> For the Lord disciplines the one he loves,
> and chastises every son whom he receives.

"It is for discipline that you endure. God is treating you as sons," he said. These saints were not to interpret their painful experiences as God's angry punishment for their sins. That angry punishment was completely spent on Jesus *once for all* on the cross.

Rather, this was the message they were to understand from their hardships: God loves you! He has fatherly affection for you. He cares deeply for you. He is taking great pains so that you will share his holiness (12:10) because he wants you to be as happy as possible and enjoy the peaceful fruit of righteousness (12:11).

This is why, as a father, whenever I discipline my children, I always try to make it clear to them that I am not paying them back for their sins. That's why I avoid using the term *punishment*. I don't want them to misunderstand and think I am giving them what they deserve. That's God's job. And if they trust in Jesus, all their punishment was taken care of on the cross.

Instead, I always use the terms *discipline* or *correction* and explain that I love them, and my intention, even though the discipline is painful, is to correct and train them. I want them to know that their father loves them, cares for them deeply, and is taking great pains to point them toward the way of joy.

It is crucial that we remember that everything God feels toward us as Christians is gracious. Even when God disapproves of sinful behaviors and habits and thoughts, and disciplines us, it is a precious form of his favor. It's what a loving father does. He is not giving us what we deserve, because he "canceled the record of debt that stood against us with its legal demands. . . nailing it to the cross" (Col. 2:14). Instead, he is training us in righteousness. Because he loves us so very much.

How long, O LORD? Will you forget me forever?
How long will you hide your face from me?

PSALM 13:1

21

HOW LONG, O LORD?

PETER TELLS US THAT "the Lord is not slow to fulfill his promise as some count slowness" (2 Pet. 3:9). At some point, each of us joins the "some" group. We reach places where it's painfully clear that our sense of time urgency must be different from God's. And it is. We prefer to measure time in minutes rather than months. But the Ancient of Days measures time by millennia (2 Pet. 3:8).

God knows that to us he sometimes appears slow, which is one merciful reason he gave us the Bible. This book, which God took millennia to assemble, shows us that God is not slow but patient in working out his redemptive purposes in the best ways (2 Pet. 3:9). And it shows that he is compassionate toward us when we wait for him for what seems like a long time.

Not as Some Count Slowness

Abraham and Sarah were not only the parents of all of God's faith children (Rom. 4:16); their lives are perhaps the most famous picture of God's redemptive purposes in what seems like his painfully slow pace.

Abram (as he was first called) was already seventy-five years old when God promised to make him a great nation that would bless all the families of the earth and to give his offspring the land of the Canaanites (Gen. 12:1–3).

However, there was a problem: Abram had no offspring. His wife, Sarai (as she was first called), was barren (Gen. 11:30).

Years passed. Still no child. So Abram prudently planned to make his servant Eliezer to be his heir. But God said, "This man shall not be your heir; your very own son shall be your heir" (Gen. 15:4). Then he took Abram out and showed him the night sky and told him that his offspring would be so numerous it would be like counting stars.

But years later, it was still just Abram and Sarai in the tent.

Sarai became desperate and gave up on waiting. She decided that her maidservant, Hagar, could be a surrogate child-bearer for her. This sounded humanly reasonable to eighty-six-year-old Abram, but he did not consult God, and the solution backfired big time.

Thirteen more years went by before God finally told the ninety-nine-year-old Abram that eighty-nine-year-old Sarai would bear a son, and he changed their names to Abraham (father of a multitude) and Sarah (princess). A year later Isaac was born.

It was twenty-five years of waiting, while any earthly reason to hope for a child went from highly unlikely to impossible. Their only hope was God's promise, which was precisely God's purpose in the long, confusing wait. "No unbelief made [Abraham] waver concerning the promise of God, but he grew strong in his faith as he gave glory to God, fully convinced that God was able to do what he had promised" (Rom. 4:20–21).

God determined that all of his true children would be born again through faith to a living hope (1 Pet. 1:3) and then they would live by faith—the faith of Abraham (Gal. 3:7)—in God's promises alone (Rom. 1:17). So he took patient pains to cultivate this faith in Abraham and Sarah, and he does the same for us.

How Long, O Lord?

One of the most profoundly comforting things about Scripture is how it reveals God's compassion for us impatient waiters. He knows that he can appear slow. He knows that at times we are going to feel like he's forgotten us and is hiding his face from us. He knows that as he patiently works out his purposes, we will experience circumstances so difficult and confusing that we cry out in bewildered pain.

And so he not only gives us stories like that of Abraham and Sarah to help us see that we are not alone; he also gives us songs like Psalm 13 to sing:

> How long, O Lord? Will you forget me forever?
> How long will you hide your face from me?
> (Ps. 13:1)

The canonical songbook is full of raw poetry—more raw and blunt than many of us are willing to be, even when confiding our pain in a trusted friend. And think about it: these were congregational songs! The people of Israel were to sing them loudly together.

And from this we are to hear from God that he knows our waiting for him can be hard. He knows it can feel to us like he is taking too long. He gives us permission to ask him things like, "How long is this going to last?" He reminds us that when we feel as though he's forgotten us, it is an experience common to all his faith children—common enough to warrant congregational singing about it.

And as we pray or sing such psalms, they remind us that God, in fact, has not forgotten us, that what we feel isn't always real, and that God's promises are truer than our perceptions.

Renewed Strength Is Coming

"The Lord is not slow to fulfill his promise as some count slowness, but is patient toward you, not wishing that any should perish, but that all should reach repentance" (2 Pet. 3:9). God's chosen pace as well as his chosen place for us—that bewildering, confusing, painful place where we feel like we're stuck—are redemptive. More than we know. There is more at stake than we can see and more going on than meets our eyes.

But here are two gracious promises God gives to us when we are waiting long:

> From of old no one has heard
>   or perceived by the ear,
> no eye has seen a God besides you,
>   who acts for those who wait for him. (Isa. 64:4)

> He gives power to the faint,
>   and to him who has no might he increases strength.
> Even youths shall faint and be weary,

and young men shall fall exhausted;
but they who wait for the LORD shall renew
their strength;
they shall mount up with wings like eagles;
they shall run and not be weary;
they shall walk and not faint. (Isa. 40:29–31)

Like Abraham and Sarah, God is working for you as you wait for him, and he will bring renewal to your weary heart.

So, "be strong, and let your heart take courage, all you who wait for the LORD" (Ps. 31:24). God will do exactly what he promised.

Do not be conformed to this world, but be transformed by the renewal of your mind, that by testing you may discern what is the will of God, what is good and acceptable and perfect.

ROMANS 12:2

22

WHY GOD'S WILL ISN'T ALWAYS CLEAR

IF GOD WANTS US to "walk in a manner worthy of the Lord, fully pleasing to him" (Col. 1:10), why doesn't he give us more specific guidance in our decisions?

The Spontaneous 95 Percent

Consider all the decisions you make during a typical day. Most are quick and spur-of-the-moment. John Piper estimates "that a good 95% of [our] behavior [we] do not premeditate. That is, most of [our] thoughts, attitudes, and actions are spontaneous."[15] That's true. And it's a bit unnerving when you think about it. The majority of the decisions that end up becoming the bricks in the building of lives are just "spill over from what's inside."[16]

Even if we do stop and pray about such decisions, it is very rare that we discern God's specific leading regarding what we should wear, what or where we should eat, if we should respond to this instance of our child's sin with correction or forbearance, if we should put off

---

15 John Piper, "What Is the Will of God and How Do We Know It?" *Desiring God* website, August 22, 2004, accessed September 28, 2015, http://www.desiringgod.org/messages/what-is-the-will-of-god-and-how-do-we-know-it.

16 Ibid.

that time-consuming errand till tomorrow, or whether
we should check our email again.

The Massive 5 Percent

But what about the other five percent of our decisions?
Some of these decisions are massive and life shaping. Should I marry this person? How much money
should I give away and where? How much should we
save for retirement? Should we adopt a child? Should
I pursue a different vocation? Should we homeschool?
Should I pursue chemo or an alternative cancer treat-
ment? Should we buy this home? Which college should
I attend? Is it time to put my elderly parent in a nursing
home? Should I go to the mission field?
Shouldn't we expect God to direct us more explicitly
in these?

A Concealing Design

The answer is no, not necessarily. Why? The short answer is that he is God, and we are not. "It is the glory
of God to conceal things" (Prov. 25:2). His wisdom and
knowledge are unfathomably deep, his judgments are
unsearchable, and his ways are inscrutable (Rom. 11:33).
Considering all the factors in play in the universe, it is
likely no exaggeration that there are trillions of reasons
for the ways God directs the course of our lives, and he
prefers to carry out his purposes in ways that confound,
surprise, and humble humans, angels, and demons.
There is a tremendous glory that God displays
when, without tipping his hand to us in advance, we

suddenly recognize that he was working his will all along when we couldn't see it. And he is also merciful to withhold information that he knows we aren't ready to know, even if we think we really want to.

A Revealing Design

But one reason that God usually doesn't give us specific guidance in our sometimes perplexing decisions is that he places a higher priority on our being transformed than our being informed in order that we will be conformed to the image of Jesus (Rom. 8:29). That's why Paul writes, "Do not be conformed to this world, but be transformed by the renewal of your mind, that by testing you may discern what is the will of God, what is good and acceptable and perfect" (Rom. 12:2).

What does this mean? It means that God has a design in the difficulty of our discerning. The sinful motives and affections of our hearts are more clearly revealed in the testing of ambiguous decision making. And forcing us to confront such sin is one of the ways he renews our minds and conforms us to the image of Christ.

In Scripture God reveals to us everything we need to know to live godly lives (2 Pet. 1:3) and to "be complete [and] equipped for every good work" (2 Tim. 3:16–17). But the Father is not seeking workers; he is seeking worshipers (John 4:23). And he knows that if he made his will for our specific decisions more explicit more often, we would tend to focus more on what we do rather than what we love. Like the Pharisees, we would tend to focus more on our actions rather than on our affections.

But in decisions that require discernment, the wheat is distinguished from the tares. When we're not quite sure, we end up making decisions based on what we really love. If deep down we love the world, this will become apparent in the pattern of decisions that we make over time—we will conform to this world.

But if we really love Jesus, we will increasingly love what he loves—we will be transformed by renewed minds. And our love for him and his kingdom will be revealed in the pattern of small and large decisions that we make.

The Pattern of Our Decisions

I say "pattern of decisions" because all of us sin and make mistakes. But conformity to the world or to Jesus is most clearly seen in the pattern of decisions we make over time.

That's one reason why God makes us wrestle with uncertainty. He wants us to mature and have our "powers of discernment trained by constant practice to distinguish good from evil" (Heb. 5:14).

The wonderful thing to remember in all of our decisions is that Jesus is our Good Shepherd. He laid down his life for us so that all of our sins are covered—including every sinful or defective decision. He will never leave us or forsake us. He has a staff long enough to pull us out of every hole and a rod to guide us back when we stray.

And someday, if we really seek to love him and trust him, we will see that he really was leading us through the confusing terrain of difficult decisions all along.

Trust in the LORD with all your heart, and do not lean on your own understanding.

PROVERBS 3:5

23

WHY THINGS OFTEN DON'T MAKE SENSE

WE HUMANS HAVE AN irrepressible need to make sense of the world and our experience in it.

Meaninglessness Is an Illusion

Darwinian naturalists believe that we adapted this need for meaning in order to secure food and pass along our genes. Nonsense. Such a belief implies that the kind of meaning that means the most to us is an illusion. And the ironic result, if we really embrace the belief that there is no meaning beyond calories and copulation, is that we neither want to eat nor pass along our genes. Meaninglessness robs us of our appetites. It makes us hate the life that our genes allegedly want above all to preserve (Eccles. 2:17).

No, we hunger for meaning because meaning exists, just like we hunger for food because food exists. Meaning is not the illusion; meaninglessness is the illusion.

The Dispelling of the Illusion

However, it is a powerful illusion. The world and our experience in it frequently do not make sense to us. Events unfold in ways that often look wrong and feel confusing. They can appear random. They can appear contrary to God's character and promises and more like the grinding gears of an indifferent cosmos. And not being able to make sense of them is very hard for us to bear and tempts us toward cynical unbelief.

But the Bible is given to us for the express purpose of dispelling this illusion. In it God reveals the great meaning that is infused into all things (Col. 1:16), the meaning that our souls hunger for and need in order to live, just like our bodies need food to live. For we do "not live by bread alone, but by every word that comes from the mouth of God" (Matt. 4:4). Meaning comes from God, and we receive it through his word.

The Most Meaningful Story

What the Bible reveals to us is that we all have the incredible, awe-filled, fearful privilege of being chosen to play a role in the greatest epic story ever conceived by the greatest Author that exists. It is the story of the glory of God (Rom. 11:36). And it is being told on such a grand scale that God must give us strength to comprehend it (Eph. 3:18). Everything in the material universe, from the most massive galaxy to the tiniest molecular particle, is involved and is itself telling a part of the story (Ps. 19:1). And there are worlds unseen to us and dimensions unknown to us that all have parts in this story (Col. 1:16). Every immaterial thought we have is part of the story (2 Cor. 10:5).

And this is the most real story that exists, for this story is reality. All the characters involved are real. All the tragedies and comedies are real. The cosmic war is as real as it gets. The stakes are real, the risks are real, the dangers are real, the punishments are real, and the rewards are real.

The story is so creative that it is by definition creation; it is so imaginative that its images are real. All our stories, all our artistic endeavors, are merely copies and shadows—pointers to or distortions of the Great Story, the Great Composition.

Why Things Appear Senseless

Is it then any wonder why things we see or experience don't make sense to us? At any given time we are seeing only a tiny, tiny fraction of the story. And the truth is, our sinful pride often leads us to a selfish myopic reading of it. We end up foolishly putting more faith in the tiny bit that we see rather than in the immense things God, the author, says.

But doesn't the Bible give us example after example after example of saints whose experience for a while—perhaps much or even all of their lives—looked wrong and yet turned out to be part of a story far larger and more meaningful than they previously imagined?

- Didn't infertility look wrong to Abraham and Sarah for decades?
- Don't you think that to Moses, whose life began with so much promise and apparent significance, shepherding another man's livestock for forty years in the Midian wilderness must have felt like a wasted life?

- Didn't Elimelech's and Mahlon's and Chilion's deaths in Moab look horrible and hopeless to Naomi (Ruth 1)?
- Didn't it look to the man born blind in John 9 (and to everyone else) like God had cursed him until Jesus showed up?
- Didn't Mary grieve over Jesus's apparent unresponsiveness to Lazarus's life-threatening illness?

There are dozens and dozens of such accounts in the Bible. And they all testify to this: *How things appear to us as characters in the story is an unreliable conveyor of meaning; we must trust the Author's perspective.*

Trust the Author

The Author is telling the story, and the Author gives each of us characters and each event more meaning than we could have imagined. What might make no sense to us today is in fact so shot through with meaning that we would be struck speechless in worshipful awe if we knew all that God was doing. And someday we will know and will worship.

The naturalistic prophets are telling you a story of meaningless despair. Do not believe their nonsense tale. That's what it is. You have a need for meaning because meaning exists. Meaninglessness is an illusion; it's a deception.

Therefore do not give in to the temptation to cynicism because you cannot yet make sense of events occurring in the world or in your own life. That is the common experience of a character in a larger story.

Trust the Author with all your heart and do not lean on your own understanding. If in all your ways you acknowledge him, he will direct you in living out most fully and fruitfully the amazing role he has given to you in this most real of all stories (Prov. 3:5–6).

Someday the Author will tell you the story in full. You will be blown away.

Look carefully then how you walk, not as unwise but as wise, making the best use of the time, because the days are evil.

EPHESIANS 5:15-16

24

YOU WILL CHANGE THE WORLD

HAVE YOU EVER WISHED you could do something that would change the world? Your wish has been granted. Are you tempted to think that your obscure, little life will leave no mark on the world? You have no idea how wrong you are.

All of History Will Be Different Because You Lived

Your very existence has already unalterably changed the course of world history. All of us—from the child who does not survive the womb to the centenarian—leave indelible marks in the lives of those around us and those who come after us. Our purposeful or incidental interactions and intersections with other people affect the timing of events or ideas or decisions that direct the future trajectory of their lives, eventually affecting millions.

Not only that, but as creatures made in God's image, God has conferred upon us the incredible dignity of being subcreators who are given real power to change the course of history through what we create. What we make with words and wood and wire and water wells and scalpels and glass and chalkboards and stone and combine harvesters and paper and glue and musical notes and motion pictures and animals and meals and photos and spreadsheets and fabrics and computer code and time with our toddler or teen and IV needles and oil paints and nails and vacuums and PVC pipe and shingles and sermons and prosthetic limbs and financial investments and welding torches and the gentle care of wounded souls is of inestimable importance and value.

Lives are changed for better or worse by how we live the life we're given and what we make with the talents we've been given. In fact, if we knew how much our lives will actually impact others and some of the unforeseen massively important things that will result from our choices, it might frighten us into near paralysis. God is merciful not to give us finite creatures foreknowledge.

No Such Thing as an Unimportant Life

There is no such thing as an unimportant, meaningless life. Life would only be meaningless if atheism were true. Then all of reality would be meaningless.

Every life God creates is good and has a purpose and therefore possesses a certain sacredness (Gen. 1:31). As stewards of the earth, we humans should approach all of life with appropriate reverence (Gen. 1:26), especially other human lives (Ex. 20:13; Matt. 5:44; 19:19).

This is one reason that abortion and euthanasia are such evils. Every life aborted at its beginning, middle, or end also alters the course of history. Whenever we take a life, another's or our own, we affect far more people than we understand.

Are you wise enough to know whether an unborn child's descendants should not live and change history?

Are you wise enough to know whether a disabled or diseased person's life has ceased to change, enrich, or direct the course of other lives? "Can you find out the deep things of God" (Job 11:7)?

There is only one who is qualified to play God, and it is his to give and take away human life (Job 1:21).

Many Who Are First Will Be Last, and the Last First

We humans are very poor judges when it comes to assessing the importance of a life. Too often we claim to be wise and show ourselves fools (Rom. 1:22). Too often we vie with others for the title "The Greatest," not understanding what greatness really is (Luke 9:46–48).

The truth is, we rarely know who the real great ones are—those whose lives prove truly great in God's assessment and bear the longest lasting fruit generations later. But we do know that Jesus said, "Many who are first will be last, and the last first" (Matt. 19:30).

Therefore, we must be careful not to "judge by appearances, but judge with right judgment" (John 7:24). And this means that we "not pronounce judgment before the time, before the Lord comes, who will bring to light the things now hidden in darkness and will disclose the purposes of the heart. Then each one will receive his commendation from God" (1 Cor. 4:5).

Live Prayerfully and Carefully with the Kingdom in View

The life you have been given is an assignment from the Lord (1 Cor. 7:17). You don't need to be someone else, and you don't need to be somewhere else. You need to be who and where God wants you to be, because your assigned life is not just about you. It's also about hundreds of others around you and hundreds of thousands of others who will come after you.

And since you are not wise or foreseeing enough to chart your own course for the sake of your present and future fruitfulness, you must follow Jesus by faith. He is your shepherd and will help you hear his voice so you can follow him in paths of righteousness for his name's sake (John 10:27; Ps. 23:3).

You will change the world more than you know. And because of that, because your life will impact so many others, Jesus wants you to live prayerfully (Eph. 6:18), walk carefully (Eph. 5:15), and seek his kingdom first (Matt. 6:33). If you do, if you faithfully invest the "little" he has entrusted to you, no labor of yours in this life will be in vain (1 Cor. 15:58), and he will entrust you with more in the life to come (Matt. 25:21).

Make love your aim.

1 CORINTHIANS 14:1, RSV

25

THE MOST COURAGEOUS RESOLUTION YOU CAN MAKE

RESOLUTIONS ARE GOOD THINGS. They're biblical: "May [God] fulfill every resolve for good" (2 Thess. 1:11). So things like New Year's resolutions can be very beneficial. A year is a defined time frame long enough to make progress on difficult things and short enough to provide some incentive to keep moving.

A resolve is not a vague intention. A vague intention is, "One of these days I'm going to get that garage cleaned," or, "I want to try reading the Bible through this year." They are vague because there are no clear plans for accomplishing them. Resolves are intentions with strategies attached. You don't just hope something is going to happen; you plan to make it happen. To be resolved is to be determined.

Make Love Your Aim

But resolves can be rooted either in our selfish ambitions or in the love of God. We must think them through carefully. So whenever we make resolutions,

God wants them all to serve this one great end: "Pursue love" (1 Cor. 14:1).

Pursue is a purposeful word. Paul chose the Greek word *diōkete*, and it is a verb with intensity. It means to "seek after eagerly," like a runner in a race seeks eagerly to win a prize, or a hunter eagerly chases his prey.

The RSV's translation of this phrase is clearer: "Make love your aim." It has a sense of single-minded focus. The NIV falls short: "Follow the way of love." It has no edge. It sounds like a platitude that polite company could smile and nod to without feeling unnerved. It does not convey Paul's intensity.

No, Paul chose an aggressive verb. In fact, *diōkete* can mean to "pursue with hostile intent." That's why in the New Testament this word is frequently used to mean "persecuting" or "harassing" someone.

That sounds like Paul, the former persecutor who became the persecuted. What he is saying to us is that we should pursue love with no less fervency and determination than he once pursued Christians to Damascus—only our aim is not to stop love but to unleash it and be captured by it, or I should say, by him (1 John 4:8).

Plan to Make Love Your Aim

Let this be the year that we pursue love. Let this be the year that we stop talking about love—that we do less regretful moaning about how little we love and how much we need to grow in love—and actually be determined to love more the way Jesus loved (John 15:12). Let this be the year we actually put into place some strategies to help us love.

Each person's situation is so unique that we can't craft strategies for each other to grow in love. It's something that we must each do with God, though some feedback and counsel from those who know us best are helpful.

But here are some of the Bible's great love texts to soak in as we prayerfully think through plans to pursue love:

- 1 Corinthians 13: Soak in or memorize it and let each "love is . . ." statement in verses 4–7 search your heart. With whom can you show greater patience, kindness, and more?
- Hebrews 13:1–7: Take one verse per day and prayerfully meditate on what you might put into place to grow in each area of loving obedience. It may be one thing or ten things.
- The Two Greatest Commandments: Take two to four weeks and simply meditate on the two greatest commandments according to Jesus (Matthew 22; Mark 12; Luke 10). Look and look at them and pray and pray over them. You will be surprised at what the Lord shows you.
- John 13–15: Soak in or memorize these chapters. Ninety-five verses are very doable. You can memorize them in three to six months and be transformed.
- The first epistle of John: Soak in or memorize it. You can do it! Forcing yourself to say the verses over and over will yield insights you've never seen before.

You get the idea. Our strategies don't have to be comprehensive or complex. Start with a couple of clear strategies and begin. And as we meditate, letting the word of Christ dwell in us richly (Col. 3:16), the Holy Spirit will guide us in creating other or better strategies. Our goal is to actually begin pursuing love with more intentionality than we ever have before.

The Most Courageous Resolution

But let's also be clear: Making love our aim will demand more courage and faith than any other resolution we can make. Nothing exposes the depth of our sin like really seeking to love God with our entire being and loving our neighbors as ourselves (Luke 10:27).

So we must let our pursuit of love drive us to the gospel. None of us has ever perfectly kept either of the two great commandments. Ever. Our very best efforts have been polluted by our prideful sin. And we have rarely been at our very best.

We can only love because God first loved us (1 John 4:19) and sent his Son to become sin for us so that we could become the righteousness of God in him (2 Cor. 5:21). Christ has kept the greatest commandments (as well as all the rest of them) perfectly for us! So we are forgiven for our constant failure to love as we ought and are given grace to grow in love. And because of Jesus, someday we will love perfectly just as we have been loved.

So let's make our resolution to pursue love this year more than we ever have, knowing that we have been loved with an everlasting love (Ps. 103:17).

You shall love your neighbor as yourself.

MATTHEW 22:39

26

LOVING THE NEIGHBOR WE DIDN'T CHOOSE

"WHO IS MY NEIGHBOR?" a lawyer asked Jesus (Luke 10:29).

The lawyer had made the mistake of trying to catch the law's Author contradicting the law by asking how he should inherit eternal life. The Author turned the tables by asking the lawyer what he thought the law said.

The lawyer then summarized the law in these two commands: We must love God with all we are (Deut. 6:5) and love our neighbor as ourselves (Lev. 19:18). The Author agreed and said, "Do this, and you will live" (Luke 10:28).

But the Author's agreement pricked the lawyer's conscience. So the lawyer sought to "justify himself" by asking, "Who is my neighbor?" (Luke 10:29). The Author answered with the parable of the good Samaritan (Luke 10:30–37).

The Neighbor We Wouldn't Choose

One observation from this application-rich parable is this: the neighbor we're called to love is often not one we choose but one God chooses for us. In fact, this neighbor is often not one we would ever have chosen had not God done the choosing.

The Jew and the Samaritan wouldn't have chosen the other as his neighbor. What made them neighbors was one man's unchosen calamity and another man's chosen compassion, but the one who chose compassion did so only in response to an unchosen, inconvenient, time-consuming, work-delaying, expensive need of another.

The shock of the parable is that God expects us to love needy strangers, even foreigners, as neighbors. But if this is true, how much more does he want us to love our actual, immediate neighbors—the ones we have to put up with regularly? Sometimes it is these neighbors we find most difficult to love. As G. K. Chesterton said,

> We make our friends; we make our enemies;
> but God makes our next-door neighbor. . . .
> The old scriptural language showed so sharp
> a wisdom when [it] spoke, not of one's duty
> towards humanity, but one's duty towards one's
> neighbor. The duty towards humanity may
> often take the form of some choice which is
> personal or even pleasurable. . . . But we have to
> love our neighbor because he is there—a much
> more alarming reason for a much more serious
> operation. He is the sample of humanity which
> is actually given us.[17]

17 Gilbert K. Chesterton, *Heretics/Orthodoxy*, Nelson's Royal Classics (Nashville: Thomas Nelson, 2000), 96.

The idea of loving our neighbor is beautiful to think about so long as it remains an idealized, abstract concept. But the concrete reality of loving our neighbor, that all-too-real, exasperating person whom we would not have chosen and might prefer to escape, strips the beauty away. Or so we're tempted to think. In truth, what usually happens is the imaginary beauty of idealized love is stripped away and the real beauty of real love is revealed in the self-dying, unchosen call to love the sinner who "is actually given us."

The Family We Didn't Choose

Our very first neighbors are in our family. We don't choose them; they are given to us. We are thrown together with them, warts and all, and called to love them—often with the kind of neighbor love Jesus had in mind. Chesterton again:

> It is exactly because our brother George is not interested in our religious difficulties, but is interested in the Trocadero Restaurant . . . [and] precisely because our uncle Henry does not approve of the theatrical ambitions of our sister Sarah that the family is like humanity. . . . Aunt Elizabeth is unreasonable, like mankind. Papa is excitable, like mankind. Our youngest brother is mischievous, like mankind. Grandpapa is stupid, like the world.[18]

18 Ibid., 98.

Many wouldn't have chosen their families if the choice had been theirs. That's why families are laboratories of neighbor love—families are a microcosm of the world.

The Community We'd Like to Un-Choose

If we are old enough and live in a region where we have options, we do choose our church community. But we don't get to choose who else joins that community.

Invariably, after some time, our church community takes on similarities to our family. We must live with leaders who disappoint us and fellow members who see the world differently. Besides their irritating temperamental idiosyncrasies, they have different interests, ministry priorities, educational philosophies, and musical preferences than we do.

"Doing life" with them doesn't end up looking or feeling like the community of our dreams—the idealized abstract imaginary community in our head. Perhaps we need a change, to find a different church where we can really thrive.

Perhaps. If the defects of the church community include things like ethical or doctrinal unfaithfulness, a change may be exactly what is needed for us to thrive.

But if our restlessness is due to the disillusionment of having to deal with difficult, different people and defective programs, then perhaps the change we need is not in church community but in our willingness to love our neighbors, the ones God has actually given us.

This has always been God's call on Christians. The early church was not all "glad and generous hearts" (Acts 2:42–47). It also had its neglected widows (Acts

6:1), divisions (1 Cor. 11:18), lawsuits (1 Cor. 6:6–8), social tensions (James 2:1–7), and sexual scandals (1 Cor. 5:1). Those first-generation churches were comprised of Jews and Gentiles, masters and slaves, rich and poor, people who preferred different leaders, people who strongly disagreed over nonessentials—people very much like the people in our church. It was hard doing life together then, like it is now (most likely it was harder then). That's why we have 1 Corinthians 13 and Romans 12.

The distinguishing mark of the church has never been its utopic society but its members' love for each other (John 13:35). And according to the parable of the good Samaritan, the glory of this love shines when it is costly and inconvenient.

"Go, and Do Likewise"

If we ask with the lawyer, "Who is my neighbor?" we may not like Jesus's answer. It may explode our dreams of love and community. Because instead of loving the neighbor we wanted, the soul mate we would have chosen, Jesus may point us to the needy, different, mess of a person in front of us—the one we feel like passing by—and say, "There is your neighbor." Perhaps he or she will be a stranger. But most likely he or she lives in our house, or on our street, or is a member of our church.

The parabolic Samaritan loved the wounded Jew as himself. And Jesus says to us what he said to the lawyer: "You go, and do likewise" (Luke 10:37).

As for me, I shall behold your face in righteousness;
when I awake, I shall be satisfied with your likeness.

PSALM 17:15

27

BEWARE THE MIRROR

MIRRORS ARE VERY DANGEROUS for proud people.

Remember the story of Narcissus? He's the proud, beautiful man in the Greek myth who saw his reflection in a pool, fell in love and couldn't tear himself away from it, and it killed him.

All of us sinners are narcissistic to some degree. But the enchanting power that mirrors have over most of us is different from Narcissus. When we look into a mirror, most of us are not captivated by our beauty. We are condemned by our defects.

And for us, mirrors are not just things that hang on our walls. Fallen, proud hearts turn just about everything into a mirror. Magazines, mall browsing, mutual fund reports, someone else's immaculate lawn or impressive children or beautiful home or successful business or growing church can all become mirrors. Because when we look at them we see reflections of ourselves. We see ourselves wanting in comparison.

So the enchantment ends up being a narcissistic obsession without changing our self-image into a thing of beauty, usually into the constantly changing, illusive images of what the world tells us is beautiful. And the power we desire our improved image to have is not to enchant ourselves by looking at our direct reflection, but to be enchanted by other people's admiration of us.

Other people's admiration is our pool of Narcissus.

This is why focusing on our self-image is so dangerous. Many of us do need our sin-corrupted, Satan-encouraged self-loathing corrected. But this will never happen by focusing on our self-image, because our salvation, peace, and happiness are not found in improving our image or having the fleeting pleasure of others' admiration. We are not designed to be satisfied with our own glory. We are designed to be satisfied with God's glory (Rom. 1:23). And however much we would like to be like God (Gen. 3:5), we never will be, not even close.

The gospel we need won't be viewed in our mirrors. For that, we need to look through a window. And that's what the Bible is. The Bible is not a mirror; it is a window. It is through the Bible that we come to see reality. And it is through the Bible that we see the "gospel of the glory of Christ, who is the image of God" (2 Cor. 4:4) and "behold, the Lamb of God, who takes away the sin of the world" (John 1:29) and "behold [his] face in righteousness" and become "satisfied with [his] likeness" (Ps. 17:15).

The health and restoration of your sin-sick, narcissistic soul lies in looking to Jesus (Heb. 12:2). It is not a better you that you need to see. You need to see Jesus and then bask in the amazing truth that the more you look to him and trust him, the more you will be conformed to his beautiful image (Rom. 8:29) and that, being in Christ, you have received and will receive as a free gift (Rom. 6:23) all that will make you most satisfied and most truly beautiful (Eph. 1:3).

Narcissus is a pagan parable of a real danger. Beware of mirrors—any kind of mirror. Look at mirrors as little as possible. Instead, look through a window. Any window is ten times more healthy for us than a mirror.

But especially look through the window of God's word so that you can see Jesus. He is the Savior (1 John 4:14), the peace (Eph. 2:14), and the satisfying gain (Phil. 3:8) you are looking for.

Believe me, the hour is coming when neither on this mountain nor in Jerusalem will you worship the Father."

JOHN 4:21

28

THE MOSQUE ON
THE MOUNT

ON THE ANCIENT TEMPLE mount in Jerusalem there
stands a mosque.

Observant Jews see a profaning of their most holy
place and plead with YHWH to remove their disgrace.
Observant Muslims see Allah's favor, a sign that the true
religion sits in ascendency.

The world sees a centuries-old religious-political
drama being played out on the edge of a knife, with
diplomats delicately working like a bomb squad to avoid
an explosion.

But most miss the real significance of the mosque
on the mount.

When the temple stood there, it was the very heart
of Judaism. It was the place where the presence of God
dwelt among his people and sacrifices were offered to
atone for sin.

But the Presence remained inside the temple, in the
Most Holy Place, cut off from sinful humans. And no
one was allowed to enter there except the high priest,
"and he but once a year, and not without taking blood,
which he offer[ed] for himself and for the unintentional
sins of the people" (Heb. 9:7).

But that all changed when Messiah appeared, as God
had promised in the Law and Prophets.

Messiah "appeared once for all at the end of the ages to put away sin by the sacrifice of himself" (Heb. 9:26). Having accomplished that, he "entered, not into holy places made with hands, which are copies of the true things, but into heaven itself . . . to appear in the presence of God" on behalf of all who would believe in him (Heb. 9:24).

Jesus became the one final sacrifice and the one final undying high priest (Heb. 7:24). He opened a "new and living way" (Heb. 10:19–20) into the most holy place in heaven for "all who would draw near to God through him" (Heb. 7:25). He became the mediator of the new covenant God had promised (Jer. 31:31–34).

At this point the presence of God moved out of the temple's holy place into his people, whom Messiah had made holy. And he began to move his people to take the gospel of the new covenant to all the peoples of the world. The Presence was moving to the peoples.

The age of the temple was over. The "copy and shadow" was "obsolete" (Heb. 8:5, 13). Therefore Jesus prophesied, "Truly, I say to you, there will not be left here one stone upon another that will not be thrown down" (Matt. 24:2). This was fulfilled in AD 70.

For the past thirteen centuries a mosque has occupied the temple's former site. It is not a sign of God's endorsement on Islam. Rather, it is an unwitting guardian of the new covenant reality. God wants the temple gone, not because Judaism is destroyed, but because in Jesus it is fulfilled.

So when you see the Al Aqsa Mosque or the Dome of the Rock, pray for both Jews and Muslims. Pray that they will hear and believe the new covenant. For "the hour [has come] when neither on this mountain nor in Jerusalem will [they] worship the Father" (John 4:21).

They were strangers and exiles on the earth.

HEBREWS 11:13

29

LIVE HOMELESS, HOMESICK, AND FREE

THERE IS A HOMELESSNESS that is distinctly Christian, because a Christian is no longer of this world, even though he or she remains in the world (John 17:14–15).

Most of us understand this abstractly. We know that Jesus chose us out of this world (John 15:19) and that Hebrews calls us to live as "strangers and exiles on the earth" (Heb. 11:13).

But the concrete experience of never quite fitting is hard to get used to. No matter where we are, no matter what we do, we're always foreigners and feel somewhat out of place.

Until we really come to grips with this reality, we will repeatedly feel disoriented and disappointed. This results in plenty of "grumbling and disputing" (Phil. 2:14) until we are willing to embrace a few realities:

- Our fallen, failing bodies are not our home. Someday they will be resurrected in perfection (1 Cor. 15:42–44), and we'll be at home in them. But right now they betray us by sin dwelling in our members (Rom. 7:23) and being subject to all manner of the futility of aging, disease, and disability (Rom. 8:20).
- Our home is not our home. No idyllic location or home improvement project will ever make our homes the heaven we seek.

- Our marriages are not our home. Marriage is a momentary parable of the permanence of Christ and the church (Eph. 5:32). But the best earthly marriages are defective parables, and most marriages are not the best. And all these earthly parables end in "till death do we part."
- Our children are not our home. Parents quickly discover childrearing to be the most difficult job in the world, all aimed at one thing: preparing our children to leave home.
- Our friendships are not our home. The best friendships go through difficult, strained seasons, and most friendships last only for brief seasons, and many end painfully.
- Our local churches are not our home. It is true that Christians are "no longer strangers and aliens, but . . . fellow citizens with the saints and members of the household of God" (Eph. 2:19). However, the New Testament Gospels and Epistles make it clear that disunity in local churches is a frequent problem (1 Cor. 1:10). Like our individual bodies, the church will one day be a perfect, glorified body of Christ (Rom. 12:5; Eph. 5:27). But right now sin, brokenness, failures, weaknesses, partisanship, doctrinal drift, sharp disagreements (Acts 15:39), and lukewarmness toward Christ all remind us that our local church is not yet our home.
- Our denominations are not our home. Very few find their family of churches a perfect fit for them. There always seems to be some doctrinal, polity, leadership, strategic, or organizational issue(s) that we find aggravating.

- Our coalitions and movements are not our home. When the Holy Spirit moves in fresh ways in the church, new coalitions and movements form to advance a Spirit-initiated mission. But it doesn't take long before the fissures of leadership frustrations, misunderstandings, selfish ambition, doctrinal differences, strategic disagreements, and criticisms remind us that we aren't home.

- Our vocations are not our home. We often spend the first half of our lives preparing for our life's work and then spend the second half of our lives trying to figure out why our life's work is not working out the way we hoped, or why it went so wrong, or why we weren't more effective, or why it was so hard.

- Our ministries are not our home. Jesus appoints us for seasons of our lives to certain responsibilities (John 3:27), and when he determines that those seasons are over, he dis-appoints us. If we were too at home in those appointments, we're left disappointed.

You Desire a Better Country

The reality we must embrace is that, like Abraham, Isaac, and Jacob, we are living in a land of promise as in a foreign land (Heb. 11:11; 2 Pet. 3:13). And like those patriarchs, but in a new-covenant sense, most of us—probably all of us—will die in faith, not having received the things promised (Heb. 11:13). And we will have no regrets because what we are really looking for is not really here.

We are "seeking a homeland"; we desire "a better country" (Heb. 11:14–16). We are strangers and exiles on earth; "here we have no lasting city, but we seek the city that is to come" (Heb. 13:14). C. S. Lewis put it beautifully: "If I find in myself a desire which no experience in this world can satisfy, the most probable explanation is that I was made for another world."[19]

The reason "home" always eludes you now is that you were made for another world. No worldly experience can satisfy your inconsolable longing. No relationship, no successful achievement, no possession, no amount of public approval will ever satisfy you here. The best these can do is give you a brief copy and shadowy glimpse of your true homeland. The best they can do is make you homesick for the better country where you belong yet have never seen.

Live Free

As a Christian, your sense of homelessness and homesickness is normal. If you've been fighting it, stop!

Embracing your homelessness as a disciple is to embrace freedom. If you don't burden your worldly experiences with the expectations of making them your home, their disappointments won't be so heavy and you'll be able to lay aside the weight of cynicism.

The really good news is that you are a stranger and exile. The more you realize this, the more it enables you to travel light. It's the cares of this world and the

---

19   C. S. Lewis, *Mere Christianity*, Kindle ed. (New York: HarperCollins, 2009), Kindle loc 136.

deceitfulness of riches that weigh you down and choke your faith (Matt. 13:22). But remembering that you don't have to make your home here will lighten your load and open your spiritual airways.

Don't worry; home is up ahead. Jesus has gone ahead of you to prepare a home for you (John 14:2). And he's made this amazing and freeing promise to you if you're willing to live "homeless": "Everyone who has left houses or brothers or sisters or father or mother or children or lands, for my name's sake, will receive a hundredfold and will inherit eternal life" (Matt. 19:29).

Don't waste precious time and resources trying to make earth your home. Instead, travel as light in your expectations and your possessions (material or emotional) as possible. And seek to take with you as many people as you can to your true homeland.

For they disciplined us for a short time as it seemed best to them, but he disciplines us for our good, that we may share his holiness.

HEBREWS 12:10

30

JESUS WILL NOT LEAVE YOU ALONE

YOU AND JESUS SHARE a desire for your comfort. But you and Jesus do not always agree on what kind of comfort is best for you.

In fact, right now you might be feeling that if Jesus really cared so much for your comfort, then you would not be dealing with such pain. But that is not true. What is true is that you likely prefer the comfort that comes from the absence of discomfort, while Jesus prefers you to have the ultimate comfort of your holiness.

So while you might feel frustrated over a very uncomfortable situation you're being forced to deal with, Jesus is actually pursuing your long-term comfort through that very situation.

It is in these seasons that Jesus's promises to be with you always (Matt. 28:20) and to never forsake you (Heb. 13:5) may not be so much comforting as they are bothersome or even painful. These are times you might wish that Jesus would just leave you alone.

But it is merciful that he does not, for unless you are holy as he is holy, you will not have the comfort you need the most (Lev. 11:44; 1 Pet. 1:16).

Training Is Always Uncomfortable

If you're a Christian, you are a disciple of Jesus. And by necessity, a disciple undergoes discipline. If a disciple is a student, then discipline is training. Jesus's discipline for you, however severe (and it is severe at times), is not God's wrath against you. If you are tempted to believe that, don't. It's your unbelief or the Enemy talking to you. When Jesus became sin for you (2 Cor. 5:21), he removed all of sin's condemnation from you (Rom. 8:1).

No, discipline is training. Training in what? Training in righteousness (2 Tim. 3:16). The unique training course that Jesus has designed for you (he designs a unique course for each disciple) has one great aim: to teach you to trust him in everything. That's his goal for you. Jesus wants you to learn to trust in him in all things at all times. For the more you trust Jesus, the holier you become.

Now, justification by faith alone is a glorious truth. When we first trust in Jesus's person and work for the forgiveness of all our sins and the promise of eternal life, God credits to us the righteousness of Christ, in union with Christ by faith. We are saved from God's wrath (Rom. 5:9), and we are considered, in that moment, holy as Christ is holy—because we are in Christ. It is a moment of great comfort.

Then comes the school of sanctification. God's ways are not our ways (Isa. 55:8). First, he confers on us the degree, and then he sends us to school. It's a wonderful education system, for we are guaranteed graduation (Phil. 1:6).

Nonetheless, in this school things get very uncomfortable for us. Jesus begins to train us to live by faith in him (Gal. 2:20). He trains us to live out the righteousness we have received through faith; he means for us to grow in the experience of the holiness he has given us; he transforms us into his likeness by the renewing of our minds (Rom. 8:29; 12:2).

Jesus Is a Gracious Trainer—and Relentless

Jesus is a gracious trainer, but he is also a relentless trainer. We are not nearly as eager for our growth in holiness as he is. We tend to think that our progress so far is good enough. We might even be tempted to think that Jesus is cruel because of the amount of pain he puts us through. But the truth is, we don't really know what's good for us.

Think of the training experiences in your life that benefitted you the most. How many of those experiences were comfortable? Zero. And the more excellence you sought (or were pushed) to achieve in a discipline, the more rigorous the training became, right?

How often did you want to give up? How often did you wonder if it was worth it? How often did you feel mad at your coach or instructor or parent or boss for pushing you beyond what you thought necessary or even possible? If you did give up, not because the training was bad for you but because you just didn't want to work at it, how did you feel? When you look back at a coach or instructor or parent or boss who just didn't let you give up on what was best for you, how do you feel about them now?

Jesus is a far better trainer than any of them. All our earthly trainers "disciplined us as it seemed best to them," but Jesus disciplines us "that we might share his holiness" (Heb. 12:10).

Jesus really does desire your comfort. He desires it more than you do. He so desires your ultimate comfort that he will make you very uncomfortable in order to give it to you.

He wants to give you the true comfort of learning to fear only God, so he will give you the discomfort of facing your false fears.

He wants to give you the true comfort of resting secure in the promises of God, so he will give you the discomfort of living with apparent uncertainty.

He wants to give you the true comfort of sharing his humility (Phil. 2:3–5), so he will give you the discomfort of opposing your pride.

He wants to give you the true comfort and joy of worshiping God alone, so he will take the painful whip of discipline into the temple of your heart to clear out the idolatrous merchants. And therefore your experience is this: "For the moment all discipline seems painful rather than pleasant, but later it yields the peaceful fruit of righteousness to those who have been trained by it" (Heb. 12:11).

Jesus, Please Do Not Leave Me Alone

So if today you're tempted to "grow weary and faint-hearted" (Heb. 12:3) in Jesus's training course for you, join me in this prayer:

Lord Jesus, forgive me for my shortsightedness and for how often I sinfully prefer my earthly comfort to the comfort of my holiness. Forgive me for the smallness of my faith. Despite what my flesh craves, my spirit craves your will for me more. I want to share your holiness and bear the peaceful fruit of righteousness. So do whatever it takes until you have completed your good work in me. For I want more than anything to trust in you in all things at all times. Please, Lord, whatever you do, do not leave me alone! I pray this in your name and for the sake of your glory. Amen.

When the perfect comes, the partial will pass away.

1 CORINTHIANS 13:10

31

WHEN THE PERFECT COMES

AT THE CLOSE OF every day, nothing is more fitting than for Christians to thank God, not only for the massive amounts of unquantifiable grace we have received from him but also because we are one day closer to the passing away of this partial age and all of its incumbent sorrow and weariness.

"When the perfect comes." Those inspired words stir up deep longings for a time we have never known and yet desperately want.

Paul may have been talking about spiritual gifts when he used that phrase in 1 Corinthians 13:10, but we know because of Romans 8 that "the partial [that] will pass away" means so much more. Right now even the best things are not what they should be. And so much goes so very wrong. In this partial age, our bodies, our loved ones, our careers, our creations, our investments, and our plans are all subject to the forces of futility (Rom. 8:20). This age is marked more by suffering (8:18), longing (8:19), groaning (8:23), and hope (8:24) than by fulfillment.

So at the day's end, especially when the pain of "the partial" has caused us groaning, let us remember that this "partial" age, all that we've ever yet known, is passing away and the perfect is coming.

To all you road-weary travelers who have found that the way that leads to life (Matt. 7:14) is harder than you ever imagined, the perfect day of rest is coming (Matt. 11:28).

To all you who find yourself poor in spirit (Matt. 5:3), humbled, desolate, and in desperate need of what only God can provide, the perfect day of the all-abundant kingdom is coming.

To all you who are mourning the loss of a precious one (Matt. 5:4) and finding it hard to press on under the heavy cloak of sorrow, the perfect day of death's death is coming (1 Cor. 15:26).

To all of you who are growing tired in the relentless struggle to hold back the flood of unrighteousness, both from within and without, and who long deeply for a time when all is made right (Matt. 5:6), the perfect day of your satisfaction is coming.

To all of you who have been injured by the maliciousness of another and have responded with a tear-filled mercy (Matt. 5:7), the perfect day of restoration is coming.

To all of you whose soft heart (Matt. 5:8) is tormented over the sin-hardened, sin-infected world around you, the perfectly pure day is coming when you will see what your soul most longs for.

To all of you peacemakers who are blessed of God (Matt. 5:9) and yet find this blessed work heartbreaking, misunderstood, and underappreciated, the perfect day of reconciliation is coming.

To all of you who find yourselves in a disorienting darkness that feels unbearable and wonder if God has abandoned you (Ps. 88:14), the perfect day is coming when the Light, in whom there is no darkness (1 John 1:5), will shine upon you (Num. 6:25).

And to all of you who increasingly love and long for Jesus's appearing (2 Tim. 4:8), who have an inconsolable homesickness for a country far better than any that exists here (Heb. 11:16), your perfect home, a home prepared especially for you (John 14:2), is coming.

When the perfect comes, the partial will pass away. The promised "soon" (Rev. 22:20) is getting sooner. Let us keep encouraging one another with these words (1 Thess. 4:18). Let us hold fast to the hope set before us (Heb. 6:18). And let us press on to know the Lord (Hos. 6:3).

Weeping may last for the night of this partial age, but joy is coming with the morning (Ps. 30:5).

GRATITUDE

MY MOTHER, MARILYN, HAS lived an epic life, though I expect she will wave this off as so much hyperbole. But it's not hyperbole. There is no ordinary life. Each life is unique. Each life is an epic. And because of the way my mother has lived her God-given epic, countless are the lives that have been enriched, comforted, and strengthened. Many are the children besides those she bore who have been cared for and housed. Many are the developmentally disabled who have heard and believed the gospel of Jesus because she had a vision to reach and teach them when most were still kept in institutions, hidden from public view. The many who know my mother know of her joy, springing from her faith in the Resurrection and the Life. But only a few really know of the immense burdens she has carried, largely in secret and without complaint, and the deep sorrows and disappointments she has endured. My mother is not impressed with herself, nor does she seek others' commendations. Recognition awards she has received over the years are in her laundry room, not her living room. They remind her of God's grace, not her greatness. She is painfully aware that she has the same sort of deceitful, desperately sick sin-nature heart as everyone else. But, thank God, my extraordinary mother did not follow her heart. She directed her heart in the way, she submitted her heart to be led by the Good Shepherd. And because of that, his heart, not hers, has governed her and she has born much good fruit. Through her remarkable example she has taught me more than she knows, and more than

I know. Therefore, it is with profound gratitude, respect, admiration, and love that I dedicate this humble book to her. I love you, Mom.

It is my incredible privilege to work with a remarkable team of very gifted ministry colleagues who serve on the board of directors and staff at Desiring God. And supporting the board and staff are remarkable donors who underwrite 98 percent of D.G.'s outreach and make it possible for this digital book to be available free. Special thanks goes to John Piper, who for twenty-four years has shared with me not only the gospel of the glory of the happy God, but his very life (1 Tim. 1:11; 1 Thess. 2:8), and to David Mathis, whose vision for this book is (humanly speaking) why it now exists. Thank you to Bryan DeWire and Lydia Brownback, whose editorial eagle eyes corrected many of my errors, and to David, Tony, Jonathan, Marshall, and Phillip, who have simply inspired me and made me a better writer, such as I am. Endless thanks goes to my priceless wife, Pam, who is my most constant source of personal human encouragement. Numerous chapters in this book were finished because she helped me.

And it will not go without saying that I owe everything to Jesus, the great shepherd of the sheep (Heb. 13:20). Thank you, Jesus, for not leaving me to follow my own lost heart but for seeking me and finding me and leading me in paths of righteousness for your name's sake (Ps. 23:3). When my flesh and heart fail, you are the strength of my heart and my portion forever (Ps. 73:26).

OTHER BOOKS
BY JON BLOOM

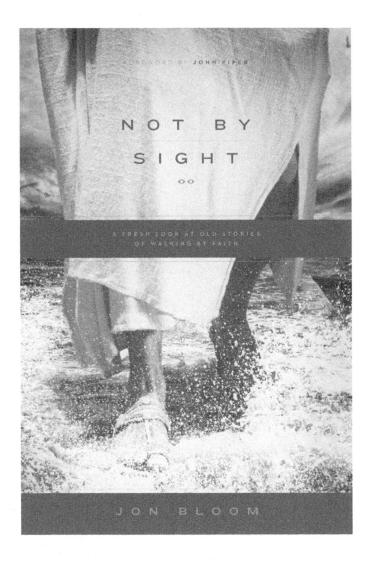

THINGS
NOT SEEN

A FRESH LOOK AT OLD STORIES
OF TRUSTING GOD'S PROMISES

JON BLOOM

⚹⚹ desiringGod

Everyone wants to be happy. Our website was born and built for happiness. We want people everywhere to understand and embrace the truth that God is most glorified in us when we are most satisfied in him. We've collected more than thirty years of John Piper's speaking and writing, including translations into more than forty languages. We also provide a daily stream of new written, audio, and video resources to help you find truth, purpose, and satisfaction that never end. And it's all available free of charge, thanks to the generosity of people who've been blessed by the ministry.

If you want more resources for true happiness, or if you want to learn more about our work at Desiring God, we invite you to visit us at www.desiringGod.org.

www.desiringGod.org

Made in the USA
Coppell, TX
04 August 2021

59933782R00108